My Pictu

Easter Island

Washington DC, USA

Pyramids, Egypt

Taj Mahal, India

re Atlas

Cape Town, South Africa

Stonehenge, UK

Venice, Italy

Sydney, Australia

Roger Priddy

priddy books

big ideas for little people

Note to parents

It is important for children to learn about every country in this wonderful, varied world, no matter how big or small and regardless of race, religion or language. For each country, this atlas gives information on population, currency and language, including how to say 'hello' wherever you are. We have also tried to include the main products that each country produces. 'Famous for' boxes for the larger countries provide information about anything from food and drink, to the culture and history of that particular place. The coloured band at the top of the page matches the fold-out map at the front of the book, so you can always find out where in the world you are.

Editorial Manager: Jo Douglass
Design Manager: Robert Tainsh
Production Manager: Louisa Beaumont
Editorial: Simon Mugford and Rebecca Clunes
Design: Jo Rigg
Illustrations: Brian Delf

With thanks

I'd like to thank my children Sam and Rose for asking the question "Where is Senegal?" The conversation that followed started the idea for this book. Also for putting up with me continuously asking questions such as, "What's the capital of Egypt?", "Where does chocolate come from?" and "How do you say hello in Thailand?"
I would also like to thank Jo and Rob for their help in taking a scribbled idea in my notebook to the book you see in front of you.
And finally to Brian Delf for his wonderful illustrations and tireless enthusiasm for the project.

We hope you enjoy this book as much as we enjoyed making it.

Contents

North America

South America

Africa

Africa

Europe

Asia

Australasia and Oceania

Earth Fact File

Continents

Asia – 43,611,165 sq km

Africa – 30,335,065 sq km

North America – 25,343,035 sq km

South America – 17,834,660 sq km

Antarctica – 13,985,935 sq km

Europe – 10,498,020 sq km

Australasia – 8,923,020 sq km

Largest Oceans

1 Pacific – 165,339,660 sq km

2 Atlantic – 82,195,860 sq km

3 Indian – 73,462,420 sq km

Longest Rivers

1 Nile (Africa) – 6,670 km

2 Amazon (South America) – 6,440 km

3 Yangtze (Asia) – 6,300 km

Highest Mountains

1 Mt. Everest (Nepal – China) – 8,848 m

2 K2 (Pakistan – China) – 8,610 m

3 Kangchenjunga (Nepal) – 8,586 m

Largest Lake

Caspian Sea (Asia) – 370,900 sq km

Largest Island

Australia – 7,617,930 sq km

Highest Waterfall

Angel (Venezuela) – 979 m

Arctic

The Arctic is a region rather than a country. It is formed from parts of Russia, Alaska, Canada, Scandinavia and Iceland. There is no solid land beneath most of the Arctic ice sheet. In summer, the ice sheet is mostly surrounded by sea. In winter, the ice extends to the mainland of the surrounding countries.

Walrus

● North Pole

Male polar bears are up to 3 metres long and are the largest predators in the world

Greenland

Nuuk

A thick layer of blubber under a seal's skin helps protect it from the icy seas

The Arctic fox is white in winter and brown in summer

Icebergs break away from the pack ice in summer and can be a hazard to ships

Famous for...

Inuit
The native people of the Arctic

North Pole
Reached by US explorer Robert Peary in 1909

Migration
Reindeer and caribou travel many kilometres between their summer and winter feeding grounds

Rich resources
Oil, copper and nickel have been found here

Canada

Canada is a very large, but sparsely populated country. Much of the northern part of the country is cold, wild and mountainous or marshy, so most people live in the large cities close to the border with the USA. Huge reserves of natural resources have made the country wealthy, with exports of oil and timber the most significant.

Canada has more lakes and waterways than anywhere else in the world. They are important transportation routes (the St. Lawrence Seaway is the world's longest and deepest inland waterway) and Canadians use them for recreation in summer and winter. Canada was settled by both the English and French and both languages are spoken.

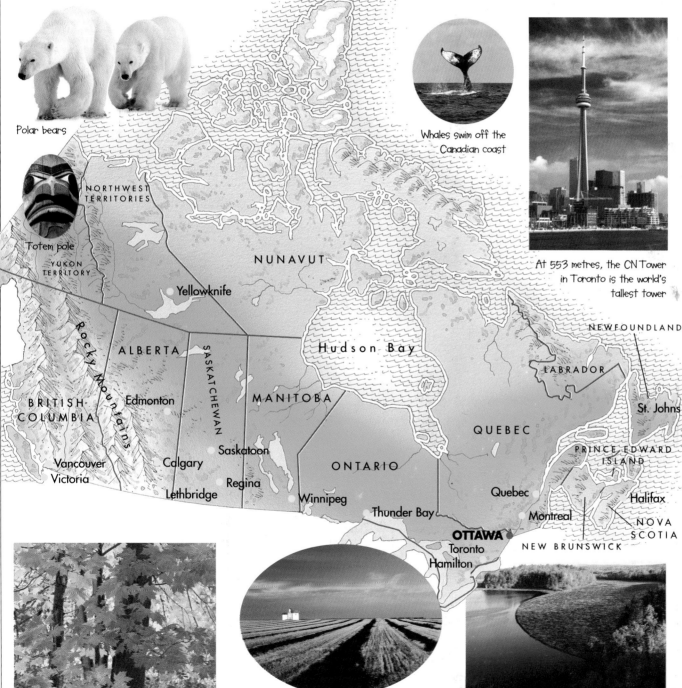

Polar bears

Totem pole

Whales swim off the Canadian coast

At 553 metres, the CN Tower in Toronto is the world's tallest tower

NORTHWEST TERRITORIES

YUKON TERRITORY

Yellowknife

NUNAVUT

Rocky Mountains

ALBERTA

SASKATCHEWAN

MANITOBA

Hudson Bay

NEWFOUNDLAND

LABRADOR

BRITISH COLUMBIA

Edmonton

Vancouver
Victoria

Calgary

Saskatoon

Lethbridge

Regina

Winnipeg

ONTARIO

Thunder Bay

QUEBEC

St. Johns

PRINCE EDWARD ISLAND

Quebec

Montreal

Halifax

NOVA SCOTIA

OTTAWA
Toronto
Hamilton

NEW BRUNSWICK

In the autumn, maple trees turn beautiful colours. The maple leaf is the national symbol

The vast prairies of western Canada are used to grow huge amounts of cereal crops

Logs are moved around by floating them on lakes and rivers

United States of America

A union of 50 states, the USA is the world's fourth largest country in area. The landscape varies enormously, from huge, flat grasslands and plains, to forests, mountains and deserts. The large number of natural resources, including fertile land for growing wheat, prairies for grazing animals and minerals like oil, gas and coal, have helped to create the most powerful economy in the world. Every major modern industry exists here, and American businesses are leaders in technology fields. The USA dominates the world's entertainment industry. Hollywood, a district of Los Angeles, has become famous as the movie-making capital of the world. America's rock and pop stars sell millions of records and its TV shows are watched in homes around the globe. All of these things make the USA a very powerful and influential country.

Mount Rushmore, South Dakota

During autumn, the leaves of New England's trees create beautiful scenery

The Statue of Liberty stands at the entrance to New York harbour

Seattle

WASHINGTON

Portland

OREGON

IDAHO

Boise

MONTANA

NORTH DAKOTA

MINNESOTA

Lake Superior

MICHIGAN

MAINE

NEW HAMPSHIRE

VERMONT

Minneapolis

WISCONSIN

Lake Huron

Lake Ontario

NEW YORK

MASSACHUSETTS

Buffalo

WYOMING

SOUTH DAKOTA

Milwaukee

Lake Michigan

Lake Erie

New York

RHODE ISLAND

CONNECTICUT

NEVADA

Salt Lake City

Rocky Mountains

COLORADO

IOWA

Des Moines

Detroit

Chicago

Pittsburgh

INDIANA

OHIO

PENNSYLVANIA

Baltimore

NEW JERSEY

DELAWARE

MARYLAND

San Francisco

UTAH

Denver

Omaha

ILLINOIS

WEST VIRGINIA

WASHINGTON DC

Las Vegas

Grand Canyon

Kansas City

St. Louis

Cincinnati

VIRGINIA

Los Angeles

CALIFORNIA

ARIZONA

NEW MEXICO

KANSAS

OKLAHOMA

Tulsa

MISSOURI

KENTUCKY

TENNESSEE

ARKANSAS

Charlotte

NORTH CAROLINA

SOUTH CAROLINA

Phoenix

Albuquerque

Memphis

Mississippi

Dallas

TEXAS

MISSISSIPPI

ALABAMA

Atlanta

GEORGIA

LOUISIANA

New Orleans

Tampa

FLORIDA

Miami

Florida grows three-quarters of the USA's oranges

Yosemite National Park in California is one of the USA's most beautiful regions

The puma is native to the western United States

San Francisco's Golden Gate Bridge is one of the world's most recognisable landmarks

The spectacular Grand Canyon in Arizona is up to 1.5 km deep in places

The White House in Washington DC is the home and office of the US president

Honolulu is the state capital of Hawaii, which lies 2,600 km out in the Pacific Ocean

States of America

 ## Alabama

A forested, woodland state where the main industry is making paper and other related products.

 ## Arizona

The vast Arizona desert is famous for its cacti. It is also home to space observatories and aircraft testing grounds.

 ## Arkansas

Major producer of cotton, rice and soya beans. The Hot Springs National Park has 47 volcanic springs.

 ## California

The most heavily populated state. Top producer of fruit and vegetables – including grapes for the wine industry.

Los Angeles is the largest city in California. More than 11 million people live there

 ## Colorado

Colorado's Rocky Mountains attract tourists all year round, for both winter sports and summer holidays.

 ## Connecticut

Known for manufacturing aeroplanes, helicopters and other military equipment.

 ## Delaware

Most of the chemical industry in the USA is based here. Also known for its clams and crabs.

 ## Florida

The 'Sunshine State'. Theme parks such as Disney World attract many visitors.

 ## Georgia

Known for growing peanuts. The world famous Coca-Cola is based in Atlanta.

 ## Idaho

Idaho grows more potatoes than any other state.

 ## Illinois

Chicago is home to some of the country's top baseball and basketball teams.

The city of Chicago is situated at the southern tip of Lake Michigan

 ## Indiana

Indiana is an important centre for making petrochemicals and pharmaceuticals.

 ## Iowa

This midwest state is famous for raising pigs and growing corn and soya beans.

 ## Kansas

The vast fields of Kansas grow more wheat than any other state.

 ## Kentucky

The 'Bluegrass State' grows lots of tobacco. The Kentucky Derby is the biggest event in US horse racing.

 ## Louisiana

Famous for the New Orleans Mardi Gras carnival. Chemical industries make use of the state's resources of oil and gas.

Louisiana's state capital, New Orleans, is famous for its jazz music

States of America

 ## Maine

The coast of Maine is well known for fishing and sailing.

Lighthouses mark hazardous areas along the rocky coast of Maine

 ## Maryland

A key shipbuilding and fishing centre. Famous for its oysters and clams.

 ## Massachusetts

Famous for Harvard University and the resorts of Martha's Vineyard and Cape Cod.

 ## Michigan

Michigan is surrounded by the Great Lakes and has many smaller lakes of its own.

 ## Minnesota

An important dairy farming state. Also known for its very cold winters and snow storms.

 ## Mississippi

The Mississippi River is a major transportation route, where goods are carried by barge.

 ## Missouri

St. Louis is the USA's largest inland port and home to the Rams American football team.

 ## Montana

Known as the 'Treasure State' because of its resources of oil, gas and precious metals.

 ## Nebraska

Cattle-farming has earned it the nickname 'Beef State'.

 ## Nevada

Known as the 'Silver State'. The city of Las Vegas is the gambling capital of the USA.

The brightly lit hotels and casinos of Las Vegas attract millions of visitors

 ## New Hampshire

Many people visit New Hampshire for its beautiful countryside.

 ## New Jersey

New Jersey grows two-thirds of the world's aubergines.

 ## New Mexico

Cattle and sheep graze the open spaces of New Mexico.

 ## New York

Apples are a major crop in New York State.

The Empire State Building is one of the most distinctive skyscrapers in New York City

 ## North Carolina

One of the major tobacco-growing states.

 ## North Dakota

Hunting elk and deer is a popular pastime in this state.

 ## Ohio

Ohio produces everything from jet engines to soap.

 ## Oklahoma

An important farming state. Tornadoes are common here.

 ## Oregon

Famous for berries, forests and salmon fishing.

States of America

Pennsylvania

Home of the Amish people and Hershey's chocolate.

Rhode Island

Smallest state in the USA. The Rhode Island Red chicken was first bred here in 1857.

South Carolina

Tobacco, cotton and corn are the main crops grown in South Carolina.

Houses like this one in South Carolina were once the homes of cotton farmers

South Dakota

The plains of South Dakota are used to grow corn and wheat and for cattle-grazing.

Hawaii

Millions of tourists travel to Hawaii – the USA's Pacific Ocean outpost.

Tennessee

Tennessee is famous for music, particularly country music.

Texas

The second largest state, with huge oil and cattle industries.

Texas farms more cattle than any other state in the USA

Utah

Utah is a leading producer of copper, gold and silver.

Vermont

Tourists flock to ski Vermont's slopes in the winter.

Virginia

One of the first parts of America to be settled.

Alaska

Alaska lies next to the northwest tip of Canada. It was bought from Russia in 1867.

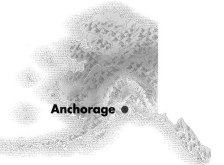

Washington

Dams along the Columbia River are used to create hydroelectric power.

West Virginia

West Virginia is a big mining state – it is the largest coal producer in the USA. It also produces fine glass.

Wisconsin

Known as 'Dairyland' because of the milk and many cheeses produced here.

Wisconsin grows lots of cranberries. Here, they are being washed and sorted

Wyoming

The landscape and wildlife of Yellowstone National Park attracts many visitors.

Famous for...

The Constitution
The United States has had the same system of government since it was formed in 1787

Hamburgers
One of the USA's most popular foods. American hamburger restaurants can be found all over the world

Disney
One of the world's largest companies, Disney's cartoons and movies have entertained children for more than 60 years

Space exploration
The USA leads the world in space exploration. It made history when it sent three astronauts to the Moon in 1969

Silicon Valley
This area of California near San Francisco is the centre of the world's computer industry

American sport
Sport is a very important part of life in the USA. American football, baseball and basketball are all popular, attracting large crowds and TV audiences

Population:	**289 million**
Money:	**US dollar**
Language:	**English**
Say hello:	**Hello**
Pronunciation:	**hel-lo**

Mexico

This large country has a varied climate, from hot, dry deserts to snow-capped mountains. Most of the steamy tropical jungles are in the southeast, and these are home to jaguars, boa constrictors and monkeys, as well as many birds. Mexico sometimes experiences volcanic eruptions and earthquakes.

Music is an important part of Mexican life. Most famous are the Mariachi bands, who wander the streets, singing and playing guitars, trumpets and violins. The 'Day of the Dead', where people remember relatives who have died, is one of a number of colourful religious festivals celebrated in Mexico.

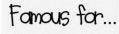

Famous for...

Chilli
Red and green chilli peppers that make Mexican food hot and spicy

Chihuahua
The smallest dog in the world. Some are small enough to stand on the palm of an adult's hand

Jumping beans
Seed pods that contain insect larvae, which make the beans move

Silver
The world's largest silver producer

Sombreros
The wide-brimmed hats

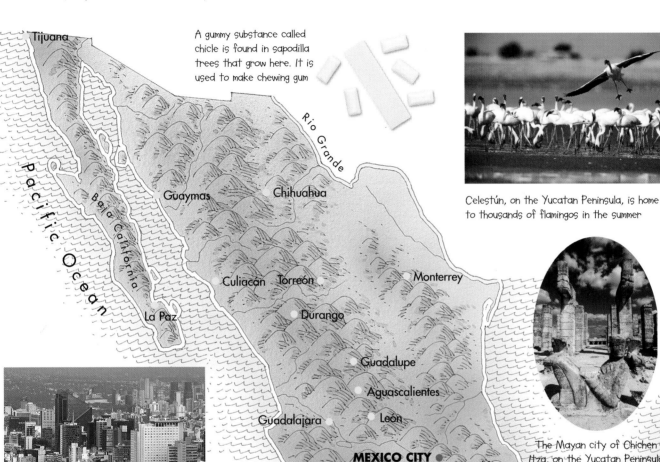

A gummy substance called chicle is found in sapodilla trees that grow here. It is used to make chewing gum

Celestún, on the Yucatan Peninsula, is home to thousands of flamingos in the summer

The Mayan city of Chichen Itza, on the Yucatan Peninsula

The capital, Mexico City, is one of the most heavily populated cities in the world

The Mayan and Aztec civilisations built many spectacular pyramids all over the country

The resort of Cancun is a popular destination for tourists from the USA

Mexican food such as burritos and fajitas are very popular all over the world

Tequila
A strong spirit made from the juice of the agave plant. Tequila is named after a town in central Mexico

Population:	**102 million**
Money:	**Mexican peso**
Language:	**Spanish**
Hello:	**Hola**
Pronunciation:	**OH-la**

St. Kitts and Nevis

Sugarcane production and tourism are the main industries on these tiny, tropical, volcanic islands.

St. Kitts

BASSETERRE

Nevis

Population:	38,800
Money:	Eastern Caribbean dollar
Language:	English
Hello:	Hello
Pronunciation:	hel-lo

Dominica

A mountainous island with lush rainforests and waterfalls. It is famous for Boiling Lake – a huge, volcanic, hot water lake.

ROSEAU

Population:	70,200
Money:	Eastern Caribbean dollar
Language:	English
Hello:	Hello
Pronunciation:	hel-lo

St. Lucia

Bananas

CASTRIES

A volcanic island with hot springs. Lots of bananas and coconuts are grown here.

Population:	160,200
Money:	Eastern Caribbean dollar
Language:	English
Hello:	Hello
Pronunciation:	hel-lo

St. Vincent
and the Grenadines

St. Vincent

KINGSTOWN

St. Vincent has an active volcano called La Soufrière. The Grenadines are made up of coral islands.

Population:	**116,400**
Money:	**Eastern Caribbean dollar**
Language:	**English**
Hello:	**Hello**
Pronunciation:	**hel-lo**

Grenada

Nutmeg

ST. GEORGE'S

Known as the 'Spice Island'. Its nutmeg trees produce half of the world's supply of nutmeg.

Population:	**89,200**
Money:	**Eastern Caribbean dollar**
Language:	**English**
Hello:	**Hello**
Pronunciation:	**hel-lo**

Barbados

The most easterly Caribbean island. A former British colony, it attracts around 500,000 tourists a year.

BRIDGETOWN

Population:	**269,000**
Money:	**Barbados dollar**
Language:	**English**
Hello:	**Hello**
Pronunciation:	**hel-lo**

Belize

Famous for...

Scuba diving
It has the second longest barrier reef in the world

Mayan ruins
Those at Lamanai on the New River date back to 1500 BC

Population:	**236,000**
Money:	**Belizean dollar**
Language:	**English**
Hello:	**Hello**
Pronunciation:	**hel-lo**

Lamanai

● **BELMOPAN**

Scuba diving

A tiny country, half of which is covered in jungle and swamps. The jungle is home to lots of animals including jaguars and toucans.

Antigua and Barbuda

Famous for...

Beaches
365, "one for every day of the year"

Sailing
In clear waters and natural harbours

Population:	**67,500**
Money:	**Eastern Caribbean dollar**
Language:	**English**
Hello:	**Hello**
Pronunciation:	**hel-lo**

Antigua has hilly regions rising to 500 metres at Boggy Peak in the south, while Barbuda is a low-lying coral island. Tourists come for the beautiful beaches.

Barbuda

● **ST. JOHN'S**

Antigua

Bahamas

Over 1.5 million tourists come here each year

Population:	**312,000**
Money:	**Bahamian dollar**
Language:	**English**
Hello:	**Hello**
Pronunciation:	**hel-lo**

● **NASSAU**

Fresh fruit

A warm sub-tropical climate, with 320 days of sunshine a year, has made the Bahamas one of the world's top holiday destinations.

Trinidad and Tobago

Trinidad and Tobago are hilly islands, with woodlands and valleys. The densely populated Trinidad has a large mountain range near its northern coast. The main exports are oil and natural gas. The country's carnival is the biggest and most popular in the Caribbean.

Calypso music, played on steel drums, was invented in Trinidad and Tobago

Tobago

● PORT-OF-SPAIN

Trinidad

Population:	1.3 million
Money:	Trinidad & Tobago dollar
Language:	English
Hello:	Hello
Pronunciation:	hel-lo

Dominican Republic

White sand beaches, forested mountains, and carnivals attract many tourists. Pico Duarte is the highest mountain in the Caribbean. Sugarcane and coffee are the country's biggest exports.

▲ Pico Duarte

● SANTO DOMINGO

School children in the Dominican Republic

Population:	8.6 million
Money:	Dominican Republic peso
Language:	Spanish
Hello:	Hola
Pronunciation:	OH-lah

Haiti

This is a very poor country, where most people are farmers who barely make enough to survive, and there is no major industry. Vetiver, a grass that is used by the perfume industry, is grown here. The country is hilly, with natural harbours.

Cap Haitien

PORT-AU-PRINCE ●

Perfume

Haiti is one of the largest producers of baseballs

Population:	8.4 million
Money:	Gourde
Language:	French
Hello:	Bonjour
Pronunciation:	bohn-ZHOOR

Costa Rica

Famous for...

Baseballs
Hand-stitched here and exported, mainly to the USA

Coffee
There are many coffee plantations producing high quality coffee beans

Population:	**4.2 million**
Money:	**Costa Rican colón**
Language:	**Spanish**
Hello:	**Hola**
Pronunciation:	**OH-lah**

Toucan in the rainforest

Costa Rica has beaches and swamps, as well as mountains covered in rainforest. It was one of the first countries to attract 'eco-tourists' – visitors who come to see the rainforest, with its thousands of types of trees, flowers and animals.

Coffee plant

Panama

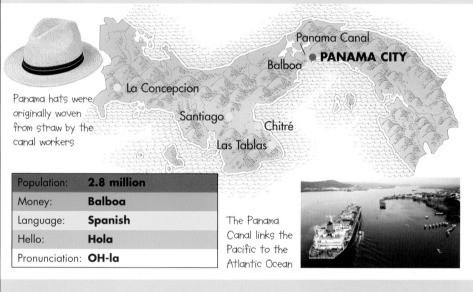

Panama hats were originally woven from straw by the canal workers

Population:	**2.8 million**
Money:	**Balboa**
Language:	**Spanish**
Hello:	**Hola**
Pronunciation:	**OH-la**

The Panama Canal links the Pacific to the Atlantic Ocean

Panama lies at the point where Central America meets South America. It also links the Pacific Ocean to the Atlantic by means of the Panama Canal (built by the USA in 1914). The canal provides ships with a short cut, saving a trip of thousands of kilometres around South America.

Nicaragua

Famous for...

Coffee
For beans used in instant coffee

Freshwater sharks
Found in Lake Nicaragua, they are the only ones in the world

Population:	**5.3 million**
Money:	**Córdoba oro**
Language:	**Spanish**
Hello:	**Hola**
Pronunciation:	**OH-la**

The largest country in Central America, Nicaragua is known as the 'land of lakes and volcanoes'. It has rainforests, mountains and fertile plains. The 160-km long Lake Nicaragua is the largest freshwater lake in the region. The Mosquito Coast is so overrun with mosquitoes, that very few people live there.

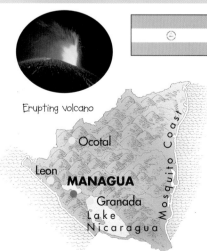

Erupting volcano

El Salvador

A small country, where volcanic ash has helped to make soil fertile. El Salvador grows coffee, sugarcane and cotton. Making cloth and clothing is an important industry. It was one of the first countries to use volcanic heat to provide electricity for homes and businesses. Many people have left rural areas to find work in cities. Football is the country's most popular sport, along with basketball and baseball.

El Salvador has many active volcanoes

Population:	6.5 million
Money:	Salvador colón/US dollar
Language:	Spanish
Hello:	Hola
Pronunciation:	OH-la

Honduras

Most people in Honduras live in small towns and villages by the coast, or in the central regions where they grow maize to make tortillas. Bananas and coffee are grown and exported around the world.
The capital's name, Tegucigalpa, means 'silver hill' after the silver found there in the 16th century. Silver is still mined here today.

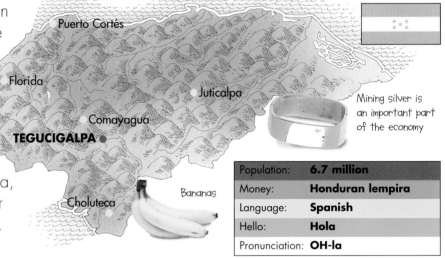
Mining silver is an important part of the economy

Bananas

Population:	6.7 million
Money:	Honduran lempira
Language:	Spanish
Hello:	Hola
Pronunciation:	OH-la

Guatemala

Guatemala is a mountainous country with dense jungles and fertile valleys. Amazing Mayan ruins and dinosaur fossils can be found here. Volcanic eruptions, earthquakes and landslides are part of life here. Guatemala's main exports are coffee, sugar and bananas. Over half of the population is under 15.

The spice cardamon is grown here and exported, mainly to Arab countries

The national bird is the beautiful quetzal. It is very rare, and was sacred to the Mayan people

Population:	12 million
Money:	Guatemalan quetzal
Language:	Spanish
Hello:	Hola
Pronunciation:	OH-la

HAVANA ●   Matanzas
     Colon
   Pinar del Rio   ● Santa Clara
   Isla de la Juventud   Cienfuegos
      Ciego de Avila
      Camagüey
      ● Holguin
      Baracoa
  Santiago de Cuba
      Guantanamo

Cuba is the largest country in the Caribbean, and its capital, Havana, is the region's largest city. It is famous for its beautiful but crumbling buildings, lively music and colourful culture. One quarter of the country is covered in mountain ranges, but most of the rest of the land is flat and fertile. Cuba's two most important exports are sugarcane and tobacco.

Cuba is home to some rare species of hummingbird

The Cuban capital, Havana, has many Spanish-style colonial buildings

Many people in Cuba drive old American cars from the 1950s and 60s

Famous for...

Cigars
Cuba has many factories making the finest cigars in the world. The tobacco leaves are picked, left to dry and then hand-rolled into cigars

Smallest bird
The world's smallest bird – the bee hummingbird – is found only in Cuba. It is actually about twice the size of a bee

Population:	**11.3 million**
Money:	**Cuban peso**
Language:	**Spanish**
Hello:	**Hola**
Pronunciation:	**OH-la**

   Montego Bay   St. Ann's Bay
     The Cockpit   Ocho Rios
     Country
      Ewarton   Port Antonio
      Blue Mountains
  Mandeville   Spanish Town   ● **KINGSTON**
     Old Harbour

Jamaica produces almost all the world's supply of allspice, which is used in spicy food

Molasses is exported to be used in cattle feed

With tropical mountains, white sandy beaches and many natural harbours, Jamaica is a popular destination for holidaymakers. Sugar production is its most important industry. Sugarcane is crushed and boiled to make sugar and molasses, which are exported. A mineral called bauxite is mined here, which is used to make aluminium. Jamaica's Blue Mountain coffee is one of the best in the world.

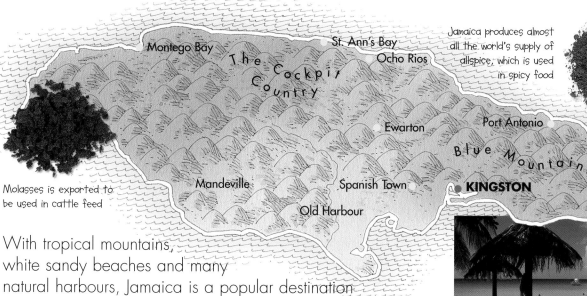

White sandy beaches and a warm climate have made Jamaica a top holiday destination

Famous for...

Reggae music
The most popular music in Jamaica. It was made famous around the world by Bob Marley

Rum
Made from molasses, and aged in oak barrels, which give it a dark colour

Jerk
Meat that has been marinated and barbecued in an outdoor pit

Population:	**2.6 million**
Money:	**Jamaican dollar**
Language:	**English**
Hello:	**Hello**
Pronunciation:	**hel-lo**

Brazil

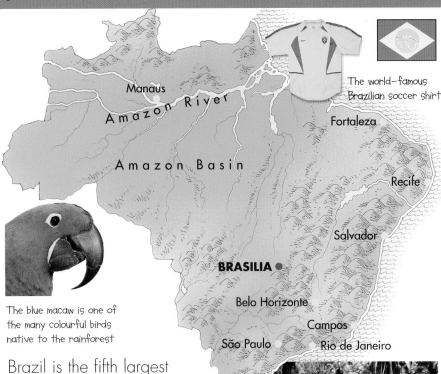

The world-famous Brazilian soccer shirt

The blue macaw is one of the many colourful birds native to the rainforest

Brazil is the fifth largest country in the world, and it covers half of South America. The Amazon River flows through the Amazon Basin in the north. This part of Brazil is covered by the largest area of rainforest in the world. It contains the most incredible variety of plants and animals anywhere on Earth. Brazil is the world's largest coffee producer. Cocoa beans (used to make chocolate) are also grown here.

The Amazon rainforest is the largest of its kind anywhere in the world

Famous for...

Football
Winners of the World Cup five times – more than any other nation

Brazil nuts
Grow in very hard shells

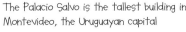

Carnival
A five-day long festival of parades, dancing and music that takes place in Rio de Janeiro

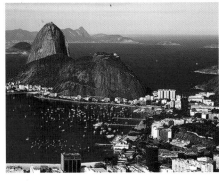
The city of Rio de Janeiro is dominated by the 400-metre high Sugarloaf Mountain

Population:	**175 million**
Money:	**Brazilian real**
Language:	**Portuguese**
Hello:	**Bom dia**
Pronunciation:	**bohn DEE-ah**

Uruguay

With low, rolling hills and plains, fertile soil and a warm climate, the prairie grassland is ideal for raising sheep and cattle. Wool and beef are Uruguay's major products, and along with leather, make up 90% of the country's exports. Beef is also an important part of the Uruguayan diet. The rhea, the largest bird in South America, is native to Uruguay.

The Palacio Salvo is the tallest building in Montevideo, the Uruguayan capital

Population:	**3.4 million**
Money:	**Uruguayan peso**
Language:	**Spanish**
Hello:	**Hola**
Pronunciation:	**OH-la**

Colombia

When the Spanish landed here in 1499, the wealth of the native Musica Indians promoted the myth of El Dorado – a mysterious city of gold. Colombia is a major coffee producer, which along with coal, is its largest export. It is named after Christopher Columbus.

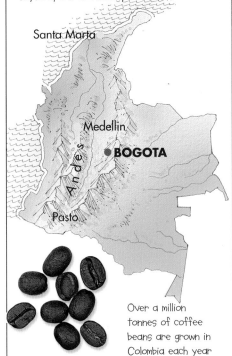

The Colombian capital, Bogota is a mix of skyscrapers and shanty towns

Over a million tonnes of coffee beans are grown in Colombia each year

Population:	**43.5 million**
Money:	**Colombian peso**
Language:	**Spanish**
Hello:	**Hola**
Pronunciation:	**OH-la**

Chile

Chile is a long, narrow country which stretches along the west coast of South America. Although it is 3,400 km long, it is rarely more than 200 km wide. The Andes Mountains stretch down the eastern edge of the country. The valleys to the south of the capital, Santiago, are fertile agricultural areas, where most of the nation's food is produced. Most of the people live in or around the capital. The Atacama Desert in the north of the country is one of the driest places in the world. Some parts of it have had no rain in recorded history.

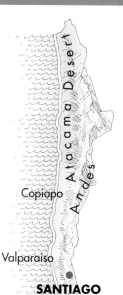

Copiapo

Valparaiso

SANTIAGO

Concepción

Valdivia

Easter Island, more than 3,000 km off the coast, is part of Chile. Hundreds of mysterious statues are found there

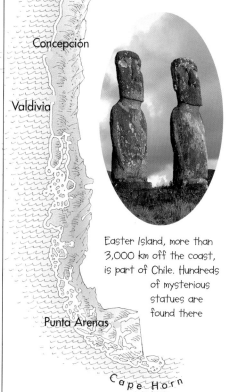

Punta Arenas

Cape Horn

Over 5 million people live in Santiago, the capital of Chile

Famous for...

Copper
The largest reserves of copper in the world

Wine
Produced in the south of the country, wine is a major export

Giant condor
The biggest flying bird in the world is found in the mountain regions

Population:	**15.6 million**
Money:	**Chilean peso**
Language:	**Spanish**
Hello:	**Hola**
Pronunciation:	**OH-la**

Many active volcanoes are found in the Andes, in the eastern part of the country

Guyana

Guyana is a small country with a tropical rainforest interior, and grassland to the southeast. 90% of the people live in the fertile coastal areas.

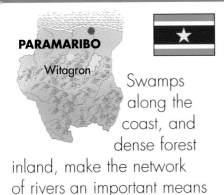

GEORGETOWN
New Amsterdam
Linden
Guyana Highlands

GUYANA   30c

SIX-BANDED ARMADILLO   *Euphractus sexcinctus*

Guyanan stamp

Population:	765,000
Money:	Guyanan dollar
Language:	English
Hello:	Hello
Pronunciation:	hel-lo

Paraguay

Gran Chaco

Concepcion

ASUNCIÓN

Encarnacion

The scrubland known as the Gran Chaco in the west makes up 60% of the land. Most people live in the east, earning a living by growing cotton and sugar, and raising cattle.

Population:	5.8 million
Money:	Guaraní
Language:	Spanish
Hello:	Hola
Pronunciation:	OH-lah

Suriname

PARAMARIBO
Witagron

Swamps along the coast, and dense forest inland, make the network of rivers an important means of transportation. 50% of the population live in the capital, Paramaribo. Aluminium, sugarcane and rice are its main exports.

Population:	421,000
Money:	Suriname guilder
Language:	Dutch
Hello:	Goedendag
Pronunciation:	goh-dehn-dahkh

Ecuador

Ecuador gets its name because it lies on the Equator. Many tourists visit the beautiful Galapagos Islands to see the unique wildlife, which includes the giant tortoise.

QUITO
Ambato
Cuenca

Giant tortoise

Population:	13.1 million
Money:	US dollar
Language:	Spanish
Hello:	Hola
Pronunciation:	OH-lah

Bolivia

LA PAZ
SUCRE
Santa Cruz
Llama

Bolivia is the most isolated country in South America. At 4,000 metres above sea level, La Paz is the highest capital city in the world.

Population:	8.7 million
Money:	Boliviano
Language:	Spanish
Hello:	Hola
Pronunciation:	OH-lah

Venezuela

Venezuela's economy is based mainly on oil. At 737 metres high, Angel Falls is the world's tallest waterfall.

Coro
CARACAS
Orinoco River
Arauca
Angel Falls

Caracas

Population:	25.1 million
Money:	Bolívar
Language:	Spanish
Hello:	Hola
Pronunciation:	OH-lah

Peru

Peru attracts many tourists because of its ancient Inca sites and breathtaking landscapes. Lake Titicaca is the world's highest navigable lake and it is the largest in South America.

Trujillo
LIMA
Machu Picchu
Cuzco
Lake Titicaca

Peruvian market

The Peruvian capital, Lima, has many beautiful Spanish colonial buildings

The spectacular, ancient Inca city of Machu Picchu lies high up in the Andes

Population:	26.5 million
Money:	New sol
Language:	Spanish
Hello:	Hola
Pronunciation:	OH-lah

Argentina

Andes
Catamarca
La Rioja
Cordoba
Santa Fe
Rosario
BUENOS AIRES
Pampas
Carmen de Patagones
Patagonia
Santa Cruz
Tierra del Fuego

Argentina is famous for its beautiful wilderness. The grasslands of Patagonia support huge flocks of sheep, while cattle are herded on the Pampas to the north – beef is an important part of the national diet and a major export. The remote, southern area of Tierra del Fuego – 'The Land of Fire' – has a large number of active volcanoes.

Magellan penguins can be seen in Patagonia

Polo is a popular sport in Argentina. It has been played here since the 19th century

Famous for...

Football
World Cup winners in 1978 and 1986

The tango
A type of ballroom dance that tells a story

Gauchos
The name for the 'cowboys' who herd cattle on the Pampas

Buenos Aires is the European-influenced, stylish and elegant capital of Argentina

Population:	37.9 million
Money:	Argentine peso
Language:	Spanish
Hello:	Hola
Pronunciation:	OH-lah

The longest mountain range in the world, the Andes, separates Argentina from Chile

Egypt

Egypt's landscape features both dry, sandy desert and green, fertile land along the Nile valley. At 6,670 km, the Nile is the longest river in world. Most of Egypt's large and growing population live along the banks of the river, which provides water for homes, businesses and farms. The Aswan Dam, which was built to prevent the annual summer flooding of the Nile, has formed the world's largest reservoir. Lake Nasser, on the border with Sudan, is 480 km long and 16 km wide. Giza is the centre of the country's significant tourism industry. This is where people come to visit the pyramids – one of the world's most recognisable landmarks. Exports of oil and natural gas are increasing, alongside established exports of fruit, vegetables and cotton – it is one of the world's largest cotton producers.

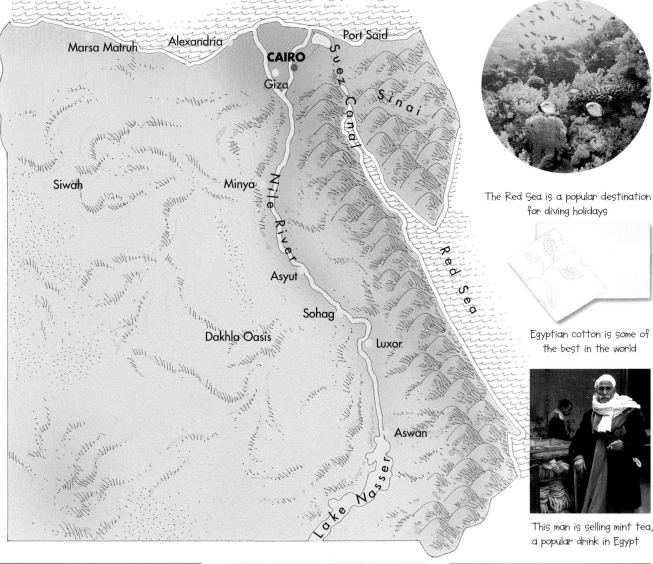

The Red Sea is a popular destination for diving holidays

Egyptian cotton is some of the best in the world

This man is selling mint tea, a popular drink in Egypt

Famous for...

Ancient Eygptians
The civilisation that rose to power about 5,000 years ago under the rule of the pharoahs

Tutankhamen
The boy pharoah's tomb, filled with incredible treasures, was discovered in 1922

Valley of the Kings
Many ancient tombs and temples were built near Luxor

Suez Canal
One of the world's most important waterways, over 10,000 ships a year pay to use it

Nile River
The longest river in the world

Mount Sinai
A mountain in the northeast of the country where, according to The Bible, Moses was given the Ten Commandments

A boat on the Nile

Population:	**70.3 million**
Money:	**Egyptian pound**
Language:	**Arabic**
Hello:	**Salaam a'alaykum**
Pronunciation:	**sah-LAHM ah ah-LAY-koom**

The pyramids at Giza are one of the world's oldest monuments, built about 2500 BC

Cairo is the largest city in Africa, with a population of more than 14.5 million

The Sphinx was probably built to guard the body of the pharoah in the largest pyramid

Morocco

Morocco has stretches of desert, snow-capped mountains and sunny beaches full of tourists. Fes and Marrakech are ancient Islamic cities with narrow, shady streets and colourful markets. Herds of animals provide hides for making leather goods.

RABAT
Fes
Casablanca
Marrakech

Cous-cous is a traditional Moroccan dish, made from wheat and flavoured with spices

Moroccan clothing and textiles are often decorated with beautiful patterns

Parts of southern and eastern Morocco are covered by the Sahara Desert

Population:	**31 million**
Money:	**Moroccan dirham**
Language:	**Arabic**
Hello:	**Salaam a'alaykum**
Pronunciation:	**sah-LAHM ah ah-LAY koom**

Chad

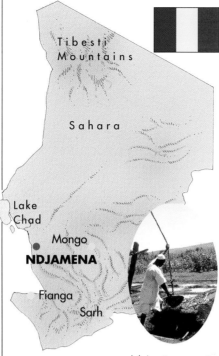

Tibesti Mountains

Sahara

Lake Chad

Mongo
NDJAMENA
Fianga
Sarh

Water is scarce in this dry country

The temperature in the desert and grasslands of northern Chad is extremely high. Most of the population live in the tropical south. Drought has caused the once enormous Lake Chad to shrink rapidly. The people have been forced to drain it to get water for their crops.

Chad is one of the poorest countries in Africa. Many people grow their own food

Population:	**8.4 million**
Money:	**CFA franc**
Language:	**Arabic**
Hello:	**Salaam a'alaykum**
Pronunciation:	**sah-LAHM ah ah-LAY koom**

Algeria

Most people in Algeria live on the strip of land near the Mediterranean coast. The rest of the country is covered by the Sahara Desert, beneath which there are rich deposits of oil.

Desert rock formations near the Ahaggar Mountains in southern Algeria

Camels are herded by the Toureg – nomads who roam the Algerian Sahara

ALGIERS
Annaba
Laghouat
Bechar
I-n-Salah
Sahara
Ahaggar Mountains

Population:	**31.4 million**
Money:	**Algerian dinar**
Language:	**Arabic**
Hello:	**Salaam a'alaykum**
Pronunciation:	**sah-LAHM ah ah-LAY koom**

Libya

Libya is one of Africa's largest countries but most of it is desert. The only green places in the desert are oases, where water from underground reaches the surface. Here, dates, olives, peaches and grapes are grown.

TRIPOLI
Ghadamis Surt Al Bayda
Libyan Desert
Ghat Sahara
Al Kufra

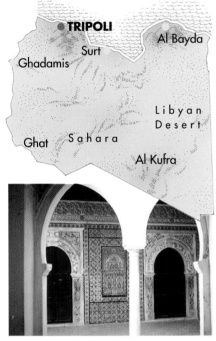

The insides of Libyan mosques are heavily decorated with mosaics

The ancient Roman city of Leptis Magna, to the east of the capital, Tripoli

Population:	**5.5 million**
Money:	**Libyan dinar**
Language:	**Arabic**
Hello:	**Salaam a'alaykum**
Pronunciation:	**sah-LAHM ah ah-LAY-koom**

Mauritania

Mauritania is one of the emptiest countries in the world. Two-thirds of it is desert, which grows bigger every year due to cattle overgrazing on the Sahel grasslands in the south. The nomadic people of Mauritania travel around the desert with their flocks of goat, sheep, camels and cattle.

Family life is especially important to nomadic people. Their families are usually very large

A cloth called a chech, worn around the head protects against sun and wind

Zouérat
Nouadhibou Sahara
Tidjikja
NOUAKCHOTT Néma
Kaedi

Population:	**2.8 million**
Money:	**Ouguiya**
Language:	**Arabic**
Hello:	**Salaam a'alaykum**
Pronunciation:	**sah-LAHM ah ah-LAY-koom**

Niger

Niger is made up of many different tribal peoples. In the north, the Tuaregs roam the Sahara. In the south, where there is more rain, the people are farmers, growing groundnuts, cotton, rice and vegetables.

Taking pots to a kiln

Sahara
Tahoua Agadez
NIAMEY Diffa

Agadez is Niger's most important desert town. The tall structure is a grain store

Camels are extremely important in Niger. They are traded at markets in major towns

Population:	**11.6 million**
Money:	**CFA franc**
Language:	**French**
Hello:	**Bonjour**
Pronunciation:	**bohn-ZHOOR**

Sudan

Sudan is the largest country in Africa. The north has a hot, desert climate, while the south is tropical. The Nile flows through Sudan, providing water to drink and to water crops. There are many different tribal and ethnic groups of people, though the country is chiefly divided between the Arabic north and African south. Sudan is a leading producer of a resin called gum arabic, which is used in soft drinks and sweets.

Sudan provides 60% of world acacia tree seedlings, used to produce gum arabic

Population:	32.6 million
Money:	Sudanese pound/dinar
Language:	Arabic
Hello:	Salaam a'alaykum
Pronunciation:	sah-LAHM ah ah-LAY-koom

Tunisia

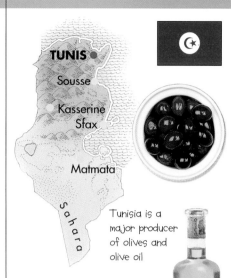

Tunisia is a major producer of olives and olive oil

The eastern end of the Atlas Mountains lie in northern Tunisia, and there are fertile plains near the coast. The Sahara Desert is in the south. Olives are Tunisia's most important agricultural product, and Tunisian olive oil is of a high quality. Other exports include tomatoes, dates and oranges. Thousands of tourists, mainly from France and southern Europe, visit Tunisia each year.

Like most north African countries, Tunisia has many craft markets, or souks

Population:	9.7 million
Money:	Tunisian dinar
Language:	Arabic
Hello:	Salaam a'alaykum
Pronunciation:	sah-LAHM ah ah-LAY-koom

Ethiopia

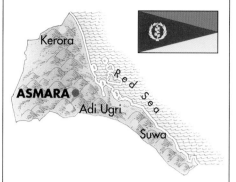

Coffee is Ethiopia's most important source of income. It is grown on plantations in the Ethiopian Highlands. Some of the best long-distance runners in the world come from Ethiopia.

Population:	66 million
Money:	Ethiopian birr
Language:	Amharic
Hello:	Tadias
Pronunciation:	tah-dee-yahs

Somalia

Old Mogadishu

Somalia is situated on the Horn of Africa, which stretches out into the Indian Ocean, and forms the Gulf of Aden. The country has suffered from years of war and famine.

Population:	9.6 million
Money:	Somali shilling
Language:	Arabic
Hello:	Salaam a'alaykum
Pronunciation:	sah-LAHM ah ah-LAY-koom

Eritrea

Eritrea means 'red', which comes from its position beside the Red Sea. It is a very poor country, where over 80% of the population are subsistence farmers or nomadic herdsmen.

Population:	4 million
Money:	Nakfa
Language:	Tigrinya
Hello:	Selam
Pronunciation:	sah-lah-ahm

Djibouti

Djibouti lies in a strategic position that links the Red Sea with the Indian Ocean. The capital, Djibouti, is an important port.

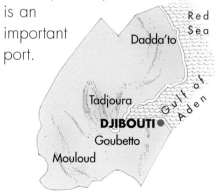

Population:	652,000
Money:	Djibouti franc
Language:	Arabic
Hello:	Salaam a'alaykum
Pronunciation:	sah-LAHM ah ah-LAY-koom

Mali

Mali is a hot, desert country. The people rely on the Niger River for fish to eat and water for crops.

Mud building

BAMAKO

Population:	12 million
Money:	CFA franc
Language:	French
Hello:	Bonjour
Pronunciation:	bohn-ZHOOR

Senegal

Most people in Senegal are farmers. The main crop grown here is peanuts.

Peanut butter

DAKAR

Population:	9.9 million
Money:	CFA franc
Language:	French
Hello:	Bonjour
Pronunciation:	bohn-ZHOOR

Gambia

The Gambia River provides the people with water for crops, fish and a means of transportation.

BANJUL

Population:	1.4 million
Money:	Dalasi
Language:	English
Hello:	Hello
Pronunciation:	hel-lo

Guinea-Bissau

Nuts are the country's most important crop. It is the world's sixth largest producer of cashew nuts.

BISSAU

Cashew nuts

Population:	1.3 million
Money:	CFA franc
Language:	Portuguese
Hello:	Bom dia
Pronunciation:	bohn DEE-ah

Guinea

Guinea is extremely hot and wet. Its resources include gold, diamonds and bauxite, which is used to make aluminium.

CONAKRY

Population:	8.4 million
Money:	Guinea franc
Language:	French
Hello:	Bonjour
Pronunciation:	bohn-ZHOOR

Sierra Leone

In tropical Sierra Leone, diamonds are the most important export. The diamonds are used in industry.

Diamonds

FREETOWN

Population:	4.8 million
Money:	Leone
Language:	English
Hello:	Hello
Pronunciation:	hel-lo

Liberia

Valuable rubber and mahogany trees grow in the Liberian forests and tropical jungle.

MONROVIA

Population:	3.3 million
Money:	Liberian dollar
Language:	English
Hello:	Hello
Pronunciation:	hel-lo

São Tomé and Príncipe

The rainforests of these tiny volcanic islands are filled with colourful canaries, parrots and kingfishers.

Príncipe
SÃO TOMÉ
São Tomé

Population:	170,400
Money:	Dobra
Language:	Portuguese
Hello:	Bom dia
Pronunciation:	bohn DEE-ah

Burkina Faso

Cotton and small amounts of gold are the main exports from this agricultural country.

OUAGADOUGOU

Population:	12.2 million
Money:	CFA franc
Language:	French
Hello:	Bonjour
Pronunciation:	bohn-ZHOOR

Ghana

Cocoa, which is used to make chocolate, is grown in Ghana.

ACCRA

Cocoa powder

Population:	20.2 million
Money:	Cedi
Language:	English
Hello:	Hello
Pronunciation:	hel-lo

Togo

Togo's main export is phosphate, a mineral used in many things, including cola drinks and antifreeze.

LOMÉ

Population:	4.8 million
Money:	CFA franc
Language:	French
Hello:	Bonjour
Pronunciation:	bohn-ZHOOR

Benin

Benin produces palm oil, which is used in ice cream, soaps and medicines.

PORTO-NOVO

Population:	6.6 million
Money:	CFA franc
Language:	French
Hello:	Bonjour
Pronunciation:	bohn-ZHOOR

Equatorial Guinea

This country is made up of mainland Rio Muni, the fertile island of Bioco and four tiny islands. Cocoa and vegetables, such as sweet potatoes, are grown here. Mahogany and other hardwoods are a major export.

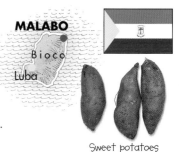

MALABO

Bioco

Luba

Sweet potatoes

Bata

Mongomo

Rio Muni

Acalayong

Population:	483,000
Money:	CFA franc
Language:	Spanish
Hello:	Hola
Pronunciation:	OH-lah

Cameroon

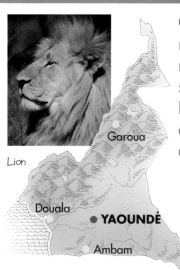

Lion

Cameroon's tropical rainforest is home to monkeys, birds and snakes, and is a source of timber. Large wild animals, including lions, elephants and antelope, roam the dry savannah grassland in the south.

Garoua

Douala

YAOUNDÉ

Ambam

Population:	15.5 million
Money:	CFA franc
Language:	English
Hello:	Hello
Pronunciation:	hel-lo

Central African Republic

The forests of this country are home to rare gorillas. This part of Africa is also inhabited by Pygmies, a race of people that grow to only about a metre tall. The Ubangi River flows along its southern border.

Ouadda

Bouar

BANGUI

Ubangi

Zinga

Fishing in the Ubangi River

Population:	3.8 million
Money:	CFA franc
Language:	French
Hello:	Bonjour
Pronunciation:	bohn-ZHOOR

Côte d'Ivoire (Ivory Coast)

The former French colony of Côte D'Ivoire is one of the largest countries on the West African coast. The climate is perfect for growing cocoa beans and 40% of the world's cocoa is produced here, making it the most important cocoa producer in the world. Coffee is also an important product for export.

YAMOUSSOUKRO

San Pedro

Chocolate

Cocoa beans

Population:	**16.7 million**
Money:	**CFA franc**
Language:	**French**
Hello:	**Bonjour**
Pronunciation:	**bohn-ZHOOR**

Gabon

LIBREVILLE

Port-Gentil

Much of the interior of the country is covered with rainforest and mountains.
The two cities of Libreville and Port-Gentil are major seaports, and most of the people live and work in them. Port-Gentil is the centre of Gabon's oil industry.

There are many rivers that run through Gabon

Population:	**1.3 million**
Money:	**CFA franc**
Language:	**French**
Hello:	**Bonjour**
Pronunciation:	**bohn-ZHOOR**

Cape Verde

Santo Antão
São Vicente
São Nicolau
Sal
Boa Vista

Cape Verde is made up of a group of volcanic islands off the coast of West Africa. Bananas are grown here for export, but most food has to be imported.

Bananas

São Tiago
Maio
Fogo
PRAIA
Brava

Population:	**446,000**
Money:	**Cape Verde escudo**
Language:	**Portuguese**
Hello:	**Bom dia**
Pronunciation:	**bohn DEE-ah**

Democratic Republic
of the Congo

This is one of Africa's largest countries. Most of the land is covered by the forests of the Congo Basin.
The Congo River is the second longest river in Africa, after the Nile. It is the main transportation route through the country.
Copper, the DRC's main export, is both mined and processed here. Copper is essential in making brass, which is used, among other things, to make some musical instruments.

Market in Kinshasa

The forests of the Democratic Republic of the Congo are home to rare mountain gorillas

Trumpet made of brass

Population:	**54.3 million**
Money:	**Congolese franc**
Language:	**French**
Hello:	**Bonjour**
Pronunciation:	**bohn-ZHOOR**

Congo

Congo is hot and humid, and covered in savannah and tropical forest.
Most of the population live in and around Brazzaville and Pointe-Noire.

The Congo River

Population:	**3.2 million**
Money:	**CFA franc**
Language:	**French**
Hello:	**Bonjour**
Pronunciation:	**bohn-ZHOOR**

Nigeria

Nigeria has the largest population of any country in Africa, and there are over 250 languages spoken here. It is a mix of a traditional African society, with people following tribal customs, and an oil-based economy with modern, western-style cities.
Nigerian oil is low in sulphur, which means it is clean, and ideal for use in jet engines.
Nigeria is always hot, but the northern savannah has very little rainfall while the southern Niger delta has rain all year round. People in rural areas grow cassava, rice, yams and maize to feed their families.

Traditional Nigerian dress

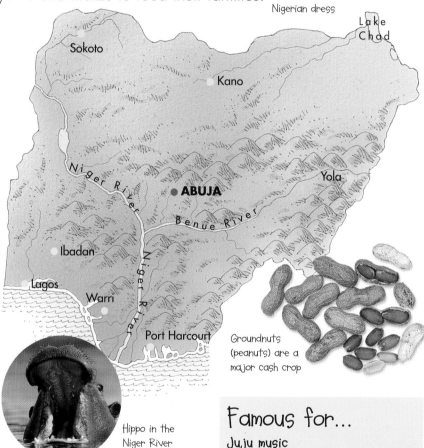

Groundnuts (peanuts) are a major cash crop

Hippo in the Niger River

Women selling spices at a Nigerian food market

Famous for...

Juju music
Has influenced western dance music

Wooden tribal masks
Used in traditional ceremonies

Football
One of the best teams in Africa

Population:	**120 million**
Money:	**Naira**
Language:	**English**
Hello:	**Hello**
Pronunciation:	**hel-lo**

Tanzania

Tanzania is home to Mount Kilimanjaro – at 5,900 metres, the highest point in Africa. There are a number of large lakes – Lake Victoria is the world's second largest freshwater lake. Many tourists visit the Serengeti region on safari to see the thousands of big game animals. The island of Zanzibar is the world's largest producer of cloves, a cooking spice.

Cloves

The central market on the island of Zanzibar. Fruits, vegetables and spices are all on sale

Rhino are among the many animals that can be seen on the Serengeti Plain

Population:	36.8 million
Money:	Tanzanian shilling
Language:	Swahili
Hello:	Jambo
Pronunciation:	JAM-bo

Malawi

LILONGWE

Malawi is dominated by the Great Rift Valley – a huge depression in the land that runs through eastern Africa. High plateaus covered in forest or savannah are found on each side of the Valley. The 353-mile long Lake Nyasa, which forms the border between Tanzania and Mozambique to the east, contains more than 500 species of fish.

Population:	11.8 million
Money:	Malawi kwacha
Language:	English
Hello:	Hello
Pronunciation:	hel-lo

Kenya

Kenya lies on the Equator. It has a tropical coastline and is hot and dry inland. Its central plain is divided by the Great Rift Valley. The country has a very productive agricultural economy, with tea and coffee being the most important exports. Kenya is the fourth largest producer of tea in world. Lots of fruit and vegetables are also grown for export. There are many national parks and game reserves, which help to protect the wild animals, and attract tourists to see them. The Masai are a nomadic tribe of people who herd cattle and goats, sharing the land with the wild animals.

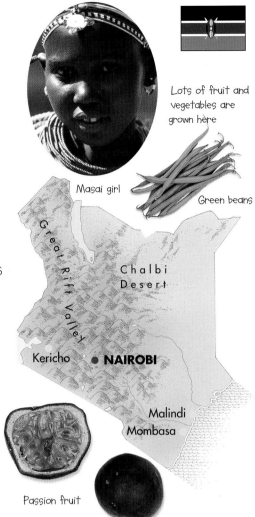

Masai girl

Lots of fruit and vegetables are grown here

Green beans

Chalbi Desert

Passion fruit

The national parks and game reserves of Kenya attract thousands of tourists

The fast-running gazelle is one of many animals that lives on the Kenyan plains

Famous for...

Wildlife
The 'big five' (lion, elephant, buffalo, rhino and leopard) can all be seen in Kenya

Long-distance running
Kenya has produced more world record holders and Olympic medallists for long-distance running than any other country

Tea
Kenyan tea is of a very high quality. Most of it is grown in the highlands around Kericho

Population:	31.9 million
Money:	Kenya shilling
Language:	Swahili
Hello:	Jambo
Pronunciation:	JAM-bo

Uganda

Arua
Lake Albert
Mbale
KAMPALA ●
Masaka
Lake Victoria

Uganda is sandwiched between the Great Rift Valley in the west and the huge Lake Victoria in the east. Most Ugandans are involved in the production of coffee – its largest export.

A royal tomb in the Ugandan capital, Kampala

Population:	**24.8 million**
Money:	**New Uganda shilling**
Language:	**English**
Hello:	**Hello**
Pronunciation:	**hel-lo**

Rwanda

Rwanda is known as the 'land of a thousand hills.' These hills are covered with coffee and tea plantations, producing the country's most valuable exports. With 300 people per square km, it is the most densely populated country in Africa.

Byumba
Lake Kivu
● **KIGALI**
Gitarama

Rare mountain gorillas live in the forests

Population:	**8.1 million**
Money:	**Rwanda franc**
Language:	**French**
Hello:	**Bonjour**
Pronunciation:	**bohn-ZHOOR**

Burundi

Muyinga
● **BUJUMBURA**
Bururi

Burundi is one of the smallest countries in Africa. Most people are subsistence farmers, where owning cattle is a sign of wealth and status. For a country of this size, there is a large mix of people from different tribes and religions.

Population:	**6.7 million**
Money:	**Burundi franc**
Language:	**French**
Hello:	**Bonjour**
Pronunciation:	**bohn-ZHOOR**

Swaziland

Swaziland is the smallest country in the southern hemisphere.
For traditional festivals, the Swazi people wear colourful costumes and perform warrior dances.

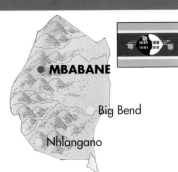

A traditional Swazi warrior dance

Population:	1 million
Money:	Lilangeni
Language:	English
Hello:	Hello
Pronunciation:	hel-lo

Lesotho

Lesotho is one of the few countries in the world to be completely surrounded by another (South Africa).
The landscape is almost entirely mountainous, earning the country the nickname 'the roof of Africa'.

A view of the Maluti Mountain Range

Population:	2.1 million
Money:	Loti
Language:	English
Hello:	Hello
Pronunciation:	hel-lo

Botswana

The Okavango is the largest inland river delta in the world, and is a haven for birds and other wildlife.
Botswana is the world's largest diamond producer.

Elephants in Botswana's Chobe National Park

Population:	1.6 million
Money:	Pula
Language:	English
Hello:	Hello
Pronunciation:	hel-lo

Angola

Angola has dry plains along its coast, and grass-covered hilly and mountainous areas inland. There are large reserves of natural resources – oil and diamonds are the country's main exports.

Over a third of the Angolan people are from the Ovimbundu tribe, who work as traders, farmers and herdsmen.

Cassava is a basic food in Angola

Population:	13.9 million
Money:	Readjusted kwanza
Language:	Portuguese
Hello:	Bom dia
Pronunciation:	bohn DEE-ah

Zambia

The Zambezi River flows along Zambia's southern border, providing water for homes and farming. Most of the country's income is gained from mining copper, although its reserves are running low.

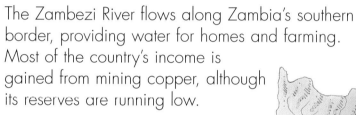

This Zambian farmer is harvesting his crops

The 100-metre high Victoria Falls are one of the most spectacular waterfalls in the world

Population:	10.9 million
Money:	Zambian kwacha
Language:	English
Hello:	Hello
Pronunciation:	hel-lo

Mozambique

There are more than 60 rivers flowing through Mozambique, including the Zambezi and Limpopo – two of the longest in Africa. The Cabora Bassa Dam on the Zambezi River is used to control the water supply to the biggest hydroelectric power plant on the continent. Most of the electricity that it produces is sold to neighbouring countries, including South Africa and Zimbabwe.

Shrimp is Mozambique's largest export

Population:	19 million
Money:	Metical
Language:	Portuguese
Hello:	Bom dia
Pronunciation:	bohn DEE-ah

Madagascar

Madagascar is the fourth largest island in the world. Its tropical rainforests attract scientists to study species of animals and plants that are found nowhere else on earth. Half of the world's supply of vanilla comes from Madagascar. The bean pods from the vanilla orchid are dried and used to flavour ice cream, chocolate and cakes.

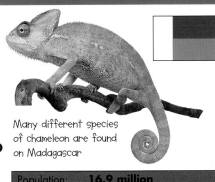

Many different species of chameleon are found on Madagascar

Sambava
Toamasina
ANTANANARIVO
Morondava
Farafangana
Toliara
Amboasary

Vanilla pods

Population:	**16.9 million**
Money:	**Malagasy franc**
Language:	**French**
Hello:	**Bonjour**
Pronunciation:	**bohn-ZHOOR**

Namibia

Thick fogs are common along the coast, but most of Namibia is extremely hot and dry. It features two deserts – the Namib and the Kalahari. The country has rich reserves of minerals, with diamonds being Namibia's most important export.

Rundu
Tsumeb
Swakopmund
WINDHOEK
Walvis Bay
Kalahari Desert
Lüderitz

Namib Desert

Namibia was the first country to make laws to protect its wildlife

Metals in the ground give the Namib desert its red colouring

Population:	**1.8 million**
Money:	**Namibian dollar**
Language:	**English**
Hello:	**Hello**
Pronunciation:	**hel-lo**

Zimbabwe

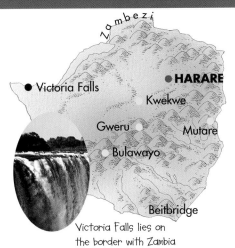

Zambezi
Victoria Falls
HARARE
Kwekwe
Gweru
Mutare
Bulawayo
Beitbridge

Victoria Falls lies on the border with Zambia

Zimbabwe's national parks and game reserves are home to some of the world's most endangered animals, including the king cheetah, and both black and white rhinos. Victoria Falls, on the Zambezi River, attracts many foreign tourists.

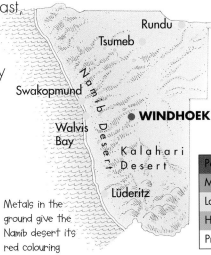

The king cheetah is the world's rarest big cat

Population:	**13.1 million**
Money:	**Zimbabwe dollar**
Language:	**English**
Hello:	**Hello**
Pronunciation:	**hel-lo**

South Africa

South Africa has an extremely varied and dramatic landscape. Spectacular mountain ranges, such as the Great Karoo in the south, and the Drakensberg in the east, separate the coast from dry, semi-desert plains and fertile land known as the veld. The temperate climate, with warm summers and cool winters, is perfect for growing fruit and vegetables, and this accounts for a large part of South Africa's economy. The country has huge resources of minerals. Mining has helped it to become the wealthiest country in Africa. It is one of the top holiday destinations in Africa, with tourists coming to see the beautiful scenery and incredible wildlife. The people are still adjusting to life after apartheid – a system that divided the country between black and white people.

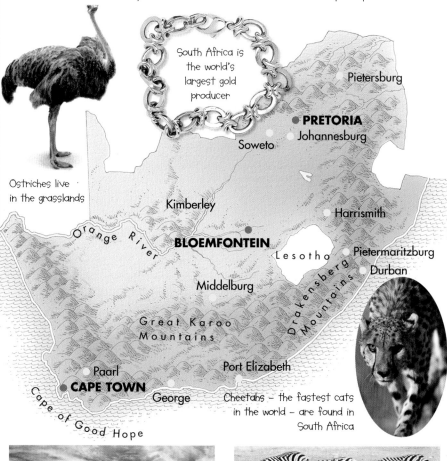

South Africa is the world's largest gold producer

Pietersburg

PRETORIA
Johannesburg
Soweto

Ostriches live in the grasslands

Kimberley
Harrismith

Orange River

BLOEMFONTEIN

Lesotho
Pietermaritzburg
Durban

Middelburg

Great Karoo Mountains

Drakensberg Mountains

Paarl
Port Elizabeth

CAPE TOWN
George

Cape of Good Hope

Cheetahs – the fastest cats in the world – are found in South Africa

Cape Town lies next to Table Mountain. Tourists can take a cable car to the top

Zebras drinking at a waterhole in one of South Africa's many game parks

Famous for...

Diamonds
Leads the world diamond market

Safari
Lions, leopards, elephants, rhinos and buffalo (the Big Five) can all be seen in South Africa

Fruit
Citrus fruits, grapes and apples are just some of the fruits that are grown here and exported

Beaches
Sunbathers and surfers consider them some of the best in the world

Rugby
The most popular sport in the country. The national team, known as the Springboks, is one of the world's best

Whale watching
Many species of whale, dolphin and shark swim close to South Africa's shores

Wine
The vineyards around Cape Town have been producing wines for centuries. Some of the best wines in the world are made here

Population:	44.2 million
Money:	Rand
Language:	Afrikaans
Hello:	Dagse
Pronunciation:	dugg-sair

Seychelles

Sandy beaches, exotic plants and animals attract tourists to this group of 115 islands in the Indian Ocean.

● **VICTORIA**

Population:	80,000
Money:	Seychelles rupee
Language:	Seselwa (French Creole)
Hello:	Bonzour
Pronunciation:	bohn-ZHOOR

Comoros

Comoros is made up of three volcanic islands. Vanilla and cloves are the main crops.

MORONI

Population:	750,000
Money:	Comoros franc
Language:	Arabic
Hello:	Salaam a'alaykum
Pronunciation:	sah-LAHM ah ah-LAY-koom

Mauritius

This mountainous, volcanic island is surrounded by coral reefs. Half the land is planted with sugarcane.

PORT LOUIS

Population:	1.2 million
Money:	Mauritian rupee
Language:	English
Hello:	Hello
Pronunciation:	hel-lo

United Kingdom

The United Kingdom is made up of four nations – England, Wales, Scotland and Northern Ireland. Separated from continental Europe by the English Channel, the climate is mild, with rain common at any time of year. The landscape is mostly lush and green. It is a major financial centre – London is home to one of world's largest stock exchanges, as well as numerous international banks and insurance companies. It is also a world leader in science, technology and medicine. The United Kingdom is one of the most densely populated countries in the world and its towns and cities are home to a mix of races from every continent. Over 25 million tourists visit the country every year, attracted by its rich history, fascinating museums, stately homes and beautiful countryside.

Fish and chips is the national dish

Lerwick

The Shetland Islands

Edinburgh Castle is the most visited tourist attraction in Scotland

Tea, taken with milk, is popular throughout the United Kingdom

The Lake District, in the northwest of England

The prehistoric monument of Stonehenge dates back to around 3000 BC

Buckingham Palace in London is the main residence of the king or queen

Stilton cheese

Strawberries

The River Thames flows through the centre of London, the capital of the UK

The west coast of the United Kingdom is rugged and beautiful

The Coldstream Guards take part in parades and ceremonies

Ireland

Famous for...

England

Sports
Football, cricket and rugby were all invented here

Shakespeare
The most famous English–language poet and playwright was born here

Channel tunnel
Opened in 1994, the 50–km tunnel provides a rail link between the United Kingdom and the rest of Europe

Northern Ireland

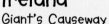

Giant's Causeway
Unusual volcanic rock formations on the northern coast

Scotland

Golf
Home to the world's oldest golf courses

Whisky
The malt–based spirit was invented here

Wales

Singing
Wales has produced many great singers

Rugby
It is the national sport of Wales

Population:	59.7 million
Money:	Pound sterling
Language:	English
Hello:	Hello
Pronunciation:	hel-lo

Ireland is known as the 'Emerald Isle' because heavy rain throughout the year makes the landscape a brilliant green colour. The plains in the centre of the country are very fertile and are used for growing wheat, barley and potatoes. The lush grass is perfect for raising animals – mostly cattle for their meat and dairy products. Ireland's inland rivers and lakes are famous for their salmon and trout fishing. They are also an important wildlife site. In the winter, ducks and geese migrate to Ireland from Greenland and Canada. The arts are very important to the Irish. They are well-known for their writers and thriving film industry. Music, often played on a fiddle or a tin whistle, is a lively part of Irish culture.

Irish rugby shirt

Donegal
Sligo
Athlone
Galway
DUBLIN ●
Irish Sea
Wicklow Mountains
Limerick
Tipperary
Tralee
Wexford
Kilarney
Waterford
Cork
Bantry

Johnstown Castle in Wexford, on the southeast coast of Ireland

The Irish are passionate about horse racing and many racehorse breeders are based here

Ha'penny Bridge, which crosses the Liffey River in Dublin's city centre

The Celtic cross is a familiar sight at religious sites across Ireland

Famous for...

Stout
Dark, almost–black beer made from roasted malt barley. The most famous stout is Guinness

St. Patrick's Day
Irish people all over the world celebrate their country's patron saint each year on March 17

Potatoes
Potatoes grow well in the wet climate of Ireland. They are the country's most important agricultural product

Population:	3.9 million
Money:	Euro
Language:	Gaelic
Hello:	Dia dhuit
Pronunciation:	jeeah-gwitch

Denmark

Denmark is a flat country, made up of the Jutland Peninsula and more than 400 other islands. Greenland and the Faeroe Islands are Danish dependencies. The climate is mild, with wet and windy winters and cool summers. Agriculture, particularly pig-farming, is an important part of the economy. Danish pork products – bacon, sausages and salami – are famous all over the world. The country also has a well-developed, high-tech economy.

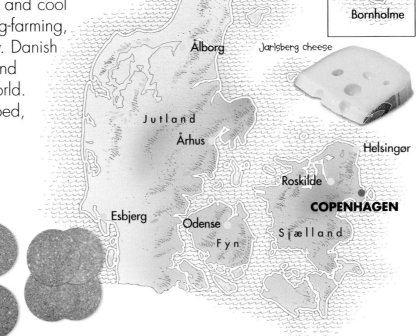

Rønne

Bornholme

Ålborg

Jarlsberg cheese

Jutland

Århus

Helsingør

Roskilde

COPENHAGEN

Esbjerg

Odense

Fyn

Sjælland

The Danish capital, Copenhagen, has many brightly-coloured old buildings

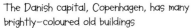

Danish salami

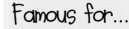
Norway

Norway has a long, rugged coastline with many islands and steep-sided inlets called fjords. The northern area inside the Arctic Circle has practically continuous daylight from May to July, but is dark almost all day during midwinter. Some of the largest glaciers in Europe are found in the mountains and there are many striking rivers, lakes and waterfalls. Oil, gas and fishing form the basis of the economy. Reindeer, wolves and polar bears can all be found in the north.

Hammerfest

Lapland

Narvik

Å

Trondheim

The northern and eastern parts of Norway experience very cold winters

Bergen

Oslo is Norway's biggest city and the oldest capital in Scandinavia

OSLO

Stavanger

Kristiansand

Norway has become Europe's largest exporter of oil and gas

Finland

Finland has over 60,000 lakes and many hills covered in forests. Timber forms the basis of the Finnish economy – papermaking and furniture production are the major industries here. The timber is transported using a canal system that links the many lakes. There is also a highly-developed telecommunications industry and many of the latest mobile phones are designed and produced here. In the spring and autumn, it is one of the best places to see the northern lights – a spectacular natural light show.

The northern lights are caused by solar winds colliding with the Earth's magnetic field

Helsinki is built on a peninsula, so many buildings face the waterfront

Finland is a world leader in mobile phone technology

Lapland

Oulu

Joensuu

Pori Tampere

Turku

Åland **HELSINKI**

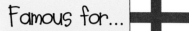

Iceland

The many active volcanoes cause spectacular geysers

Vatnajökull in the southern half of the country, is the biggest glacier in Europe

Iceland is the most western island in Europe. There are huge glaciers, hot springs, geysers and active volcanoes. Geothermal energy is used to provide free heating for Icelanders. Fishing is the most important industry.

Population:	**283,000**
Money:	**Icelandic krona**
Language:	**Icelandic**
Hello:	**Hallo**
Pronunciation:	**hal-lo**

Estonia

Estonia is a flat, boggy country with some pine and spruce forests. The forests are home to many rare animals, including the European flying squirrel. Lake Peipus, on the border with Russia, is one of the largest lakes in Europe. Much of the agriculture is based around potatoes and raising brown pigs.

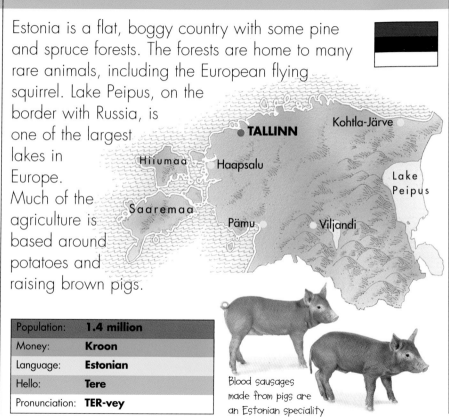

Population:	**1.4 million**
Money:	**Kroon**
Language:	**Estonian**
Hello:	**Tere**
Pronunciation:	**TER-vey**

Blood sausages made from pigs are an Estonian speciality

Sweden

Beautiful lakes are common here

In the winter months, Sweden's rolling hills are covered in snow and its many lakes and rivers ice over. Skiing and skating are popular winter pastimes. There is a strong, industrial based economy, with companies producing cars, aircraft, mobile phones, and other high-tech products. Sweden's economic success has made it a wealthy country, and its people enjoy one of the highest standards of living in the world. Large forests produce wood, used for making furniture and paper. The many rivers provide the country with a means of producing hydroelectric power.

Traditional houses have steeply sloping roofs so that snow will sllide off in winter

The Swedish capital, Stockholm, is an important seaport

Famous for...

Alfred Nobel
Set up the foundation that awards prizes for peace, science and literature

Mobile phones
Sweden is a leading producer of mobile phones

Pippi Longstocking
The popular books, written by Astrid Lindgren, which have been translated into 60 languages

Furniture
Known for its very well designed products. IKEA is one of Sweden's most successful companies

Population:	8.8 million
Money:	Swedish krona
Language:	Swedish
Hello:	God dag
Pronunciation:	goo dahg

Latvia

There is a large otter population in Latvia

Much of Latvia is low-lying swampy land with many rivers and lakes. To grow crops, the land has to be drained. Most Latvian meals contain fish – the most popular are smoked flounder, eel and herring. Peat cut from the bogs is used as fuel and fertiliser.

Population:	2.4 million
Money:	Lats
Language:	Latvian
Hello:	Labdien
Pronunciation:	lub-dean

Lithuania

Most of the world's amber (the fossilised sap of ancient trees), is supplied by Lithuania. Sheets of amber lie on the bed of the Baltic Sea and stormy weather washes it onto the country's 'Amber Coast'. Flax is grown on the flat, fertile land. Flax fibres are used to make rope, footwear and fine linen.

Amber

The Holy Spirit Church in Vilnius is one of the most impressive in the country

Population:	3.7 million
Money:	Litas
Language:	Lithuanian
Hello:	Labas
Pronunciation:	lah-bahs

Netherlands

The Netherlands are also known as Holland, but strictly speaking this is just the area around Amsterdam. It is a very flat land, much of which is below sea level. For centuries, barriers called dykes have been used to keep out the sea and reclaim some of the land. Agriculture and food processing makes up a large part of the Dutch economy and even small, family-run farms are highly mechanised. Rotterdam is Europe's biggest seaport, with over 30,000 ships using the port each year. Its position allows ships easy access to the Rhine River, which is an important trade route into northern Europe. Dutch electronics, especially televisions and stereos, are famous worldwide for their high quality.

Dutch beer is famous the world over

Cheese, such as Gouda, is a major Dutch export

- Groningen
- Friesland
- Den Helder
- Alkmaar
- Haarlem
- **AMSTERDAM**
- Zwolle
- Enschede
- **THE HAGUE**
- Utrecht
- Arnhem
- Rhine
- Rotterdam
- Maas
- Middelburg
- Breda
- Tilburg
- Eindhoven
- Flushing
- Maastricht

Famous for...

Artists
Dutch painters Rembrandt and Vincent Van Gogh are two of the best known artists in history

The black and white Friesian cow comes from Friesland. It is an excellent dairy cow

Royal family
The royal family is well-loved throughout the Netherlands. The official residence is the Huis ten Bosch Palace near The Hague

Skating
Ice skating is a popular pastime

Two capitals
Amsterdam is the capital city, but the government is based in The Hague

Tulips
The brightly-coloured flowers are exported all over the world

Windmills
Many windmills can be seen across the flat Dutch landscape

The Hague is home to the Dutch government and the International Court of Justice

Diamonds are brought to Amsterdam to be cut and polished. The city specialises in the diamond trade

Football is popular, and the national team is well-supported

Population:	**16.2 million**
Money:	**Euro**
Language:	**Dutch**
Hello:	**Goedendag**
Pronunciation:	**goh-dehn-dahkh**

The flat countryside and many cycle routes have made travelling by bike very popular

Amsterdam is built on many islands and is one of the world's great canal cities

Many tourists visit the country in the spring to see fields of beautiful flowers

Belgium

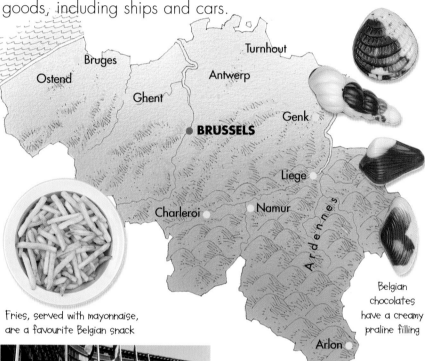

Belgium is a country with flat, fertile plains in the north and the rugged Ardennes Mountains in the south. The country is divided between two peoples – the Flemings in the north, who speak Flemish, and the French-speaking Walloons in the south. Belgium has few natural resources, but it imports raw materials to make a range of industrial goods, including ships and cars.

Mussels

Turnhout
Bruges
Ostend
Ghent
Antwerp
Genk
● BRUSSELS
Liege
Charleroi
Namur
Arlon
Ardennes

Fries, served with mayonnaise, are a favourite Belgian snack

Belgian chocolates have a creamy praline filling

The headquarters of the European Union (EU) is based in Brussels

Bruges is one of the best preserved medieval cities in Europe

Famous for...

Mussels
Mussels, usually served with fries, is a very popular dish

Lace
Some of the world's finest lace is made in Brussels and Bruges

Diamonds
Antwerp is the centre of the world's industrial diamond industry

Saxophone
Invented here in the 1840s

Population:	**10.3 million**
Money:	**Euro**
Language:	**Flemish**
Hello:	**Goede morgen**
Pronunciation:	**khoodemohrg'n**

47

Luxembourg

Luxembourg is a tiny industrialised country with the highest standard of living in Europe. There are many castles and medieval villages. The Ardennes Mountains are a popular destination for skiers and there are many vineyards in the Moselle Valley.

A square in the town of Echternach

Population:	**448,000**
Money:	**Euro**
Language:	**French**
Hello:	**Bonjour**
Pronunciation:	**bohn-ZHOOR**

Liechtenstein

This tiny country is only 30 km long and 8 km wide. It lies between the Rhine valley and the foothills of the Tirolean Alps. Much of the country is forested. International banks attract foreign workers, mainly from Germany and Switzerland. Its main exports are dental products, furniture, chemicals and stamps. Skiing is a popular tourist activity in the winter.

Population:	**32,800**
Money:	**Swiss franc**
Language:	**German**
Hello:	**Guten Tag**
Pronunciation:	**GOOT-en tahk**

Monaco

Monaco has been ruled by the Grimaldi family for about 700 years. It is a major business centre and attracts very rich visitors.

Monaco is famous for its casinos, yacht harbour and Grand Prix racing circuit

Population:	**32,000**
Money:	**Euro**
Language:	**French**
Hello:	**Bonjour**
Pronunciation:	**bohn-ZHOOR**

France

Famous for...

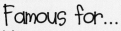

Wine
France produces about a quarter of the world's wine. Champagne is made in the area around Reims

Perfume
Scented grasses and flowers are grown to make some of the world's finest perfumes

Croissants
Freshly baked breads or pastries that are eaten for breakfast

Tour de France
The gruelling, month-long cycling race takes place across France's varied countryside, including steep mountains. People line the streets to cheer the cyclists as they pass through towns and villages

Café culture
The tradition of visiting cafés to eat, drink and meet people began in France in the 17th century. Cafés are now popular all over the world

Film
Moving pictures, projected onto a screen, were invented here by the Lumière brothers in 1895

Film festival
A famous film festival is held each year in Cannes

Population:	**59.7 million**
Money:	**Euro**
Language:	**French**
Hello:	**Bonjour**
Pronunciation:	**bohn-ZHOOR**

The French TGV train carries passengers at up to 300 kilometres per hour

Lavender, used in perfumes, is grown around Grasse in southern France

The long, slim French bread is famous worldwide

The Arc de Triomphe in Paris was built to honour the Emperor Napoleon

A typical tree-lined avenue in the beautiful Rhône Valley, in southern France

The French landscape includes the mountains of the Pyrenees and Alps, the rocky coastline of Brittany, and the Mediterranean beaches of the southern coast. It is one of the world's leading agricultural countries, producing a wide range of farm products. Cereal crops are grown on a large scale in the area around Paris. France is highly industrialised, with oil refining, steel production and chemical processing among its industries. It also has western Europe's second largest car manufacturing industry, mostly based in Paris. The French people have a long tradition of elegance and style and Paris continues to be a world leader in the fashion industry.

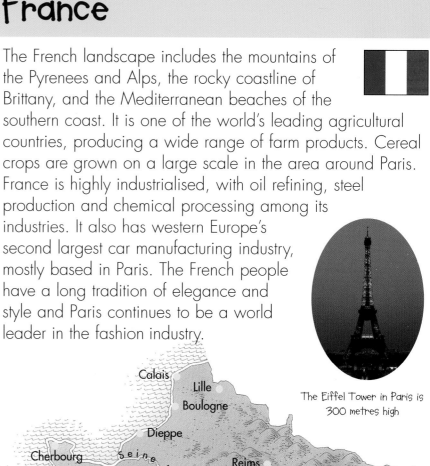

The Eiffel Tower in Paris is 300 metres high

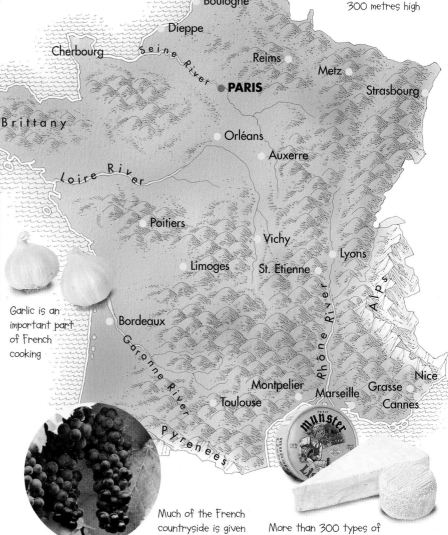

Garlic is an important part of French cooking

Much of the French countryside is given over to vineyards

More than 300 types of cheese are made in France

Spain

Spain is the third largest country in Europe and includes the Balearic and Canary Islands. Mountains dominate much of the Spanish landscape, from the Pyrenees on the border with France and the Sierra Nevada in the south, to the Cantabrian Mountains in the northwest. Spain is one of the world's largest producers of olives and olive oil.

The olives are harvested by beating the trees with sticks. Some crops, such as tomatoes and strawberries, are grown on irrigated land. It is the leading European producer of metals, including iron ore, lead and copper. Fishing is an important industry along the northern coast. Fleets of boats spend months in fishing grounds far from shore.

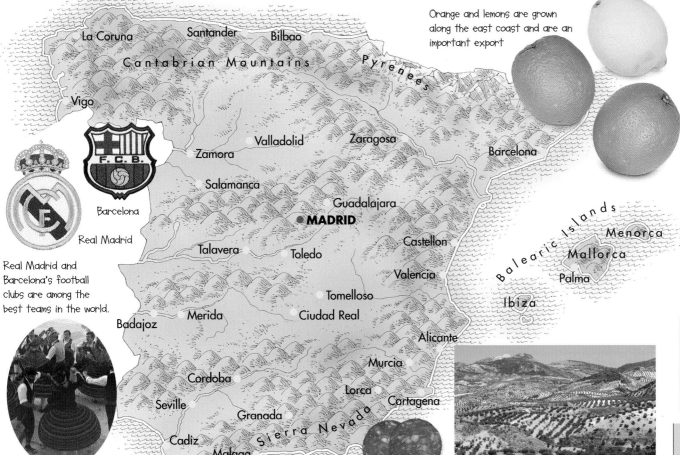

Orange and lemons are grown along the east coast and are an important export

Real Madrid and Barcelona's football clubs are among the best teams in the world.

The south is the home of the flamenco dance and music

Spicy chorizo sausage is a popular food

Much of the south and east of Spain is taken up by huge olive groves

Madrid is full of beautiful buildings such as the Palace of Communications

The Sagrada Familia Cathedral is one of the most famous sights in the city of Barcelona

Spain's many sandy beaches attract millions of tourists from all over Europe

Andorra

The principality of Andorra lies high in the Pyrenees between France and Spain. Many people visit to go skiing.

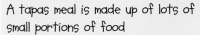

Portugal

Portugal has rugged hills in the north, where the climate is cool and rainy (it has the most rainfall in western Europe). The south is flat with very little rain. Most people live in the north and in the central regions where there are forested mountains, deep valleys and many rivers. There are many vineyards and groves of olive, almond, fig and orange trees. Fishing is a very important industry, and the largest catch is sardines. The most popular way of eating sardines them is to have them grilled. Other important industries include textile production, winemaking and manufacturing footwear, all of which are exported throughout Europe and the world.

Sardines are canned and exported all over the world

Seafood such as shrimp is caught off the Portuguese coast

Lisbon is an important port that lies at the mouth of the Tagus River

The coastal area of Algarve is popular with tourists from across Europe

The rolling hills of the Portuguese landscape, dotted with olive trees

The Jerónimos Monastery is one of Lisbon's most impressive buildings

The Azores

Madeira

Famous for...

Cork
Portugal is the world's leading producer of cork. It is waterproof and airtight and is used for flooring and winestoppers

Port
Port is a fortified wine made in the valley around the Douro River

Explorers
Ferdinand Magellan, the first person to sail around the world, was one of several well-known explorers to come from Portugal

Population:	**10 million**
Money:	**Euro**
Language:	**Portuguese**
Hello:	**Bom dia**
Pronunciation:	**bohn DEE-ah**

Greece

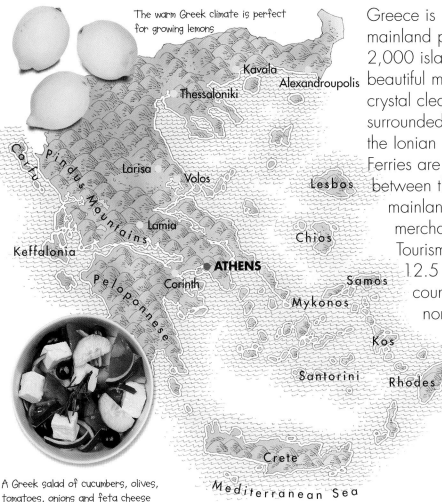

The warm Greek climate is perfect for growing lemons

Kavala
Alexandroupolis
Thessaloniki
Corfu
Pindus Mountains
Larisa
Volos
Lesbos
Lamia
Chios
Keffalonia
Peloponnese
ATHENS
Corinth
Samos
Mykonos
Kos
Santorini
Rhodes
Crete

Mediterranean Sea

A Greek salad of cucumbers, olives, tomatoes, onions and feta cheese

Greece is made up of a mainland peninsula and 2,000 islands known for their beautiful mountain landscapes and crystal clear waters. The country is surrounded by three seas – the Aegean, the Ionian and the Mediterranean. Ferries are an important means of travel between the many islands and the mainland. Greece has the largest merchant ship fleet in the world. Tourism is a huge industry – over 12.5 million people visit the country each year, mainly from northern Europe. Tourists come to the island resorts and to visit the ruins of ancient Greece.

Famous for...

Olives
Olives have been grown in Greece for more than 2,000 years

Olympics
The games began in ancient Greece. The first modern Olympics were held in Athens in 1896

Mount Olympus
The highest point in Greece (2,970 metres). It was thought to be the home of gods in ancient times

Taramasalata
A creamy paste made from fish eggs, olive oil, lemon juice and garlic. It is a popular snack

Population:	**10.6 million**
Money:	**Euro**
Language:	**Greek**
Hello:	**Kalimera**
Pronunciation:	**kah-lee-MEH-rah**

Many very old windmills can be found on the island of Mykonos

Ferries are the main way of travelling between the Greek islands

Zakynthos is one of the Ionian islands which are very popular with tourists

The Parthenon, an ancient temple, lies on top of a hill called the Acropolis in Athens

Italy

Italy is mostly mountainous, with the Alps in the north and the Apennines running along the length of the country. The northern region, around the cities of Milan and Turin, is where most of the country's industry is located, while the south is mainly agricultural. Italy is a world leader in stylish design, especially for cars and clothes – Milan is widely regarded as the fashion capital of the world. Tourism is a hugely important industry, with millions of tourists coming to visit ancient Roman sites and historic cities such as Venice, Naples and Florence.

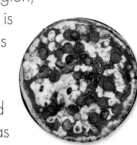
Italy is the home of pizza

Coffee is very popular in Italy

Pisa's world famous leaning tower

Parmesan cheese comes from the region around Parma

Famous for...

Wine
Italy has been making wine for thousands of years and is the world's largest wine producer

Ferrari
The world famous sports cars are made in Modena

Art
Some of the world's most important works of art were made by Italian artists such as Michaelangelo and Leonardo da Vinci

Football
Italians are passionate about football and have some of the best teams in the world

Pasta, in all its various forms, is one of the world's most popular foods

Positano is a town of a brightly coloured villas perched on steep cliffs

The unique city of Venice is famous for its canals and many historical buildings

The Colosseum in Rome is one of the city's many ancient Roman sites

Population:	57.4 million
Money:	Euro
Language:	Italian
Hello:	Buon giorno
Pronunciation:	bwohn JOR-noh

San Marino

The tiny Republic of San Marino is built on the steep slopes of Mount Titano and is completely surrounded by Italy. The capital itself is an ancient fortress with steep cobbled streets. It is one of the venues for Grand Prix races.

Population:	27,000
Money:	Euro
Language:	Italian
Hello:	Buon giorno
Pronunciation:	bwohn JOR-noh

Vatican City

The world's smallest independent state is situated in the centre of Rome. It is the capital of Roman Catholicism and home to the Pope.

St. Peter's Basilica in Vatican City is one of the most visited religious sites in the world

Population:	900
Money:	Euro
Language:	Italian
Hello:	Buon giorno
Pronunciation:	bwohn JOR-noh

Germany

Germany has the largest population in Europe and is the wealthiest country on the continent. Most people live in Germany's many cities and large towns. There are low plains in the north, rolling forested hills in the centre and the Bavarian Alps in the south. The Rhine is Germany's major river, providing a transportation route for cargo across Europe. Germany is a world leader in science and technology, with large exports of cars, electronics and other industrial goods. It has also led the way in producing 'green' products that cause less harm to the environment.

Beer is brewed in most major towns and cities

Kiel
Rostock
Lübeck
Hamburg
Bremen
Elbe River
Hanover
BERLIN
Münster
Duisburg
Dortmund
Dusseldorf
Kassel
Leipzig
Cologne
Erfurt
Dresden
Bonn
Frankfurt
Rhine River
Nuremberg
Stuttgart
Black Forest
Munich
Bavarian Alps

Sausages are a very popular food here

Clear rivers, high mountains and unspoilt woodland are features of the Black Forest

Frankfurt is the business capital. Many international companies have offices here

Germany makes some of the best cars in the world

German bread is heavy and dark in colour

Famous for...

Classical music
Bach, Beethoven and Wagner are among the great German classical music composers

Electrical goods
Germany leads the world in the production of large electrical goods such as washing machines

Berlin Wall
Germany was once divided between east and west. The wall across the capital that symbolized the divide was torn down in 1989

Cakes
Chocolate and fruit cakes made in Germany are popular all over the world

Wine
The most popular German wine is reisling

Population:	**82 million**
Money:	**Euro**
Language:	**German**
Hello:	**Guten Tag**
Pronunciation:	**GOOT-en tahk**

There are many beautiful castles in the southern region of Bavaria

A traditional house in the Black Forest, in the southwest of the country

The Brandenburg Gate is at the point that divided east and west Berlin

Switzerland

The Alps dominate Switzerland, making up over 60% of the land. The highest mountain is Monte Rosa at 4,633 metres, although the better known Matterhorn and Eiger are more spectacular. Heavy winter snows in the mountains make it one of Europe's top skiing destinations. Banking and other financial services are very important to the economy, as is the manufacture of small, precisely engineered items such as clocks and watches.

Zurich

Neucahtel

Lucerne

•BERN

Lausanne

▲Eiger

Montreux

Geneva

▲ Matterhorn

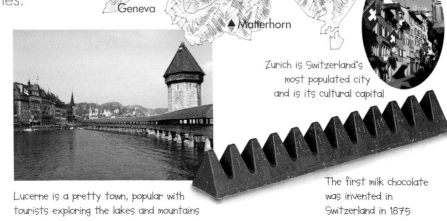

Zurich is Switzerland's most populated city and is its cultural capital

The first milk chocolate was invented in Switzerland in 1875

Mountaineers from all over the world take up the challenge of climbing the Matterhorn

Lucerne is a pretty town, popular with tourists exploring the lakes and mountains

Famous for...

Skiing
Many of the world's top skiers are Swiss

Red Cross
This international aid agency was set up in Switzerland in 1863

Swiss army knife
This consists of many blades and implements that can be folded down into the handle

Watches and clocks
Swiss clocks are known for their accuracy

Population:	**7.2 million**
Money:	**Swiss franc**
Language:	**French**
Hello:	**Bonjour**
Pronunciation:	**bohn-ZHOOR**

Austria

Majestic mountains and deep valleys in the south and west of Austria make up 70% of the country. Ibex (mountain goat) and chamois (antelope) can be found here. Austria is one of Europe's most heavily wooded countries, with forests of oak, beech and conifer. At 2,000 metres the trees give way to mountain meadows. Mountain rivers generate hydroelectric power for much of the country.

Linz
Danube **VIENNA**
Baden
Gmunden
Salzburg
Leoben
Innsbruck **A l p s**
Graz
Klagenfurt

Famous for...

Vienna Boys Choir
For 500 years the Choir has been known for its beautiful singing

Lipizzaner horses
These pure white horses perform in a special show in Vienna

Composers
Mozart, Haydn, Schubert and the Strauss family come from Austria

Graphite
Mined here and used to make the lead in pencils

Population:	**8.1 million**
Money:	**Euro**
Language:	**German**
Hello:	**Gruß Gott**
Pronunciation:	**groose gott**

The Hohensalzburg Fortress in Salzburg is the largest of its kind in Europe

Tourists go hiking in the Austrian Alps in the summer and skiing in the winter

The lakeside village of Hallstatt is one of the oldest in Austria

Poland

Poland's flat land is perfect for growing crops. To the south the land gets hillier, and beneath the hills of Katowice lies one of the world's largest coal fields. Coal provides energy for the iron and steel mills which in turn provide the metal for Poland's many machine-building factories. Storks are a familiar sight in many Polish villages. They build their nests on roofs and chimneys.

The Old Town in Warsaw was completely rebuilt after the Second World War

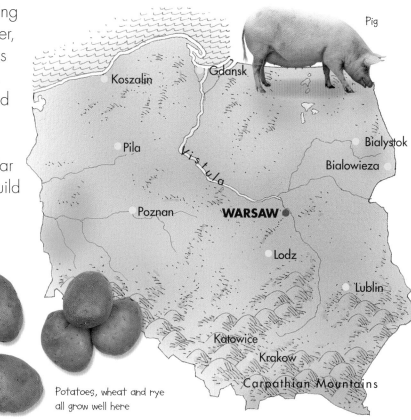

Pig

Potatoes, wheat and rye all grow well here

Famous for...

Salt pork
Used in many traditional dishes

Bigos
'Hunter's stew' is a favourite, filling meal

Vodka
The national alcoholic drink

Bison
European bison can be found in Bialowieza National Park

Zinc
Mined in the south of the country and used in batteries

Population:	**38.3 million**
Money:	**Zloty**
Language:	**Poland**
Hello:	**Czesc**
Pronunciation:	**chesht**

Czech Republic

This popular tourist destination has warm summers and cold, snowy winters. The different styles of buildings in the capital, Prague, have made it one of Europe's most beautiful cities. The Czech region of Bohemia is famous for glassmaking. Glass is made by melting sand, soda and limestone. It is then painted, engraved or cut into intricate designs. The glassmakers produce jewellery and stained glass windows as well as fine drinking glasses.

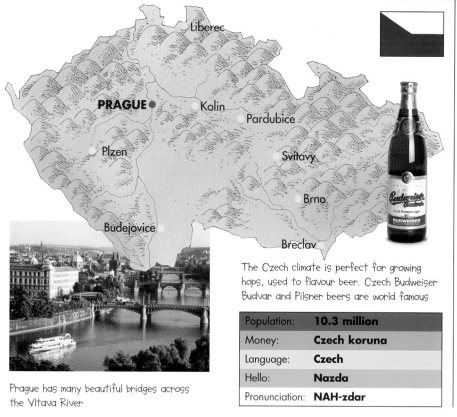

Prague has many beautiful bridges across the Vltava River

The Czech climate is perfect for growing hops, used to flavour beer. Czech Budweiser Budvar and Pilsner beers are world famous

Population:	**10.3 million**
Money:	**Czech koruna**
Language:	**Czech**
Hello:	**Nazda**
Pronunciation:	**NAH-zdar**

Slovakia

The High Tatras mountain range is popular for skiing and hiking. The High Tatras is also home to wolves, lynxes, chamois and mink. Slovaks are proud of their traditional dress and music.

Population:	**5.4 million**
Money:	**Slovak koruna**
Language:	**Slovak**
Hello:	**Nazdar**
Pronunciation:	**NAH-zdar**

Belarus

Belarus has the largest marshlands in Europe and forests of silver birch, pine, oak and beech which provide timber for building and papermaking. Mushroom picking is popular. Any mushrooms that are not eaten immediately are dried, salted or pickled for use throughout the winter. Mushroom and barley soup is a speciality.

Mushrooms grow in the thick forests

Some of the more remote and untouched forests are home to wild elks

Population:	**10.1 million**
Money:	**Belarussian rouble**
Language:	**Belarussian**
Hello:	**Pryvitannie**
Pronunciation:	**pri-VEET-an-nyyeh**

Ukraine

Sugar

Ukraine is one of the most fertile places on earth. Huge quantities of wheat, rye, oats and sugar beet are grown on Ukraine's vast, rolling plains. Beneath the rich black soil lie other treasures – coal and metal ores. The coal provides energy for Ukraine's iron, steel and machine-building industries. The Donbass Basin is Europe's largest coalfield. Ukraine is a centre of sugar production.

St Andrew's Church in Kiev is topped with five spectacular domes

Population:	**48.7 million**
Money:	**Hryvna**
Language:	**Ukrainian**
Hello:	**Pryvit**
Pronunciation:	**pri-veet**

Hungary

Budapest is the lively capital city

Hot summers and mild winters make Hungary suitable for growing all kinds of crops. Almost half of the world's paprika comes from here. Budapest is actually two cities, Buda and Pest, which lie on either side of the Danube River. This river flows through 10 countries.

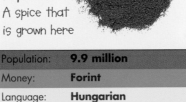

Famous for...

Goulash
Beef and vegetable stew spiced with paprika

Holograms
Invented by the Hungarian Denis Gabor. He received the Nobel Prize in 1971

Paprika
A spice that is grown here

Population:	**9.9 million**
Money:	**Forint**
Language:	**Hungarian**
Hello:	**Szia**
Pronunciation:	**ZEE-yah**

Romania

This land of fairytale castles, medieval cities and mountain forests is also one of the poorest in Europe. Most people work on farms and many people still travel by horse and cart.

Many Roma (gypsies) live in Romania. These nomadic people have a long tradition of music, horse-training and acrobatics. The legend of Count Dracula is based on Vlad the Impaler, who was born in the medieval town of Sighisoara.

Home-grown fruits and vegetables can be found in many small markets

Population:	**22.3 million**
Money:	**Romanian leu**
Language:	**Romanian**
Hello:	**Buna ziua**
Pronunciation:	**BOO-nuh ZEE-wa**

Bulgaria

Rose petals are sent to distilleries to make attar

Bulgaria is popular with tourists. They come for the dramatic mountains, golden beaches and ancient Roman ruins. Bulgaria's healthy climate, clear warm seas and mineral springs are thought to cure many illnesses. Roses are grown to make attar, an oil used in perfume. Shoes and boots made in Bulgaria are exported across Europe.

Vineyards thrive in Bulgaria's climate, and red wine is exported around the world

Population:	7.8 million
Money:	Lev
Language:	Bulgarian
Hello:	Dobur Den
Pronunciation:	dob-ur den

Serbia and Montenegro

This country is divided into two republics, Serbia and Montenegro, plus the United Nations controlled area of Kosovo. During the long winter months, skiing is popular. When the snow melts, the Tara River is the place to go white-water rafting. The Djerdap Gorge in the Carpathian Mountains has one of Europe's largest hydroelectric plants.

There are traditional costumes for each region of Serbia and Montenegro

Population:	10.5 million
Money:	Dinar/Euro
Language:	Serbo-Croat
Hello:	Zdravo
Pronunciation:	zdrah-voh

Slovenia

Slovenia is a hilly country covered in forest. Hiking and skiing in the mountains are popular. Slovenia has some very deep caves beneath its mountains and many unique animals can be found in them.

Population:	2 million
Money:	Tolar
Language:	Slovene
Hello:	Zivjo
Pronunciation:	zhee-vee-yo

Croatia

Many people visit Croatia's beautiful rocky Adriatic coast and its 1,185 islands. Split has one of the finest Roman ruins in the world – a palace built in 295 AD.

Dalmations were first bred here

Population:	4.7 million
Money:	Kuna
Language:	Croatian
Hello:	Zdarvo
Pronunciation:	ZDRAD-vo

Bosnia and Herzegovina

This country has beautiful lakes and forests. The population is made up of three groups: the Serbs, Croats and Bosnian Muslims.

Population:	3.9 million
Money:	Convertible mark
Language:	Serbo-Croat
Hello:	Zdravo
Pronunciation:	zdrah-voh

Macedonia

This green and beautiful land experiences frequent earth tremors and earthquakes. Tobacco is Macedonia's main crop.

Tobacco

Population:	2.1 million
Money:	Macedonian denar
Language:	Macedonian
Hello:	Prijatno
Pronunciation:	pree-yat-no

Moldova

Lipcani

CHISINAU

Cahul

Sunflowers and grapes grow well in the mild climate

Cereal, vegetables and fruit are important exports, while oil is a major import. Carpet weaving has been an art form here for centuries.

Population:	**4.3 million**
Money:	**Moldovan leu**
Language:	**Moldovan**
Hello:	**Buna ziua**
Pronunciation:	**BOO-nuh ZEE-wa**

Cyprus

There are many ancient ruins and castles on Cyprus. Greek Cypriots live in the southern part of the island while Turkish Cypriots live in the north. It has a long history of lace-making.

NICOSIA

Ayia Napa

Potatoes and citrus fruits grow well on the island

Population:	**797,000**
Money:	**Cyprus pound**
Language:	**Greek**
Hello:	**Kalimera**
Pronunciation:	**kah-lee-MEH-rah**

Turkey

Turkey is a land of rocky coastlines, grassy plains, mountains and fertile valleys. Flocks of sheep are raised on the central plains to produce lamb's wool for making Turkey's famous carpets. Angora goats, from Ankara, have long wavy hair which is used to make mohair. Cotton, grown in western Turkey, is used by American and European fashion designers.

Lamb's wool is soft and strong

Istanbul

Bursa

ANKARA

Izmir

Konya

Adana

Nuts and dried fruit are a popular snack here

Famous for...

Shish kebabs
The Turkish way of grilling lamb on skewers

Turkish delight
A sweet made from sugar and gum

Belly dancing
An ancient fertility dance still popular at Turkish weddings

Turkish rugs
Good quality carpets, noted for being colourful and stylish

Turkish baths
Half an hour in hot steam followed by body brushing, dousing in cold water and then a relaxing massage

Albania

Albania has rugged mountains and beautiful beaches, where rare Dalmatian pelicans can be seen. Summers here are hot and dry. The economy is mainly agricultural, with some mineral exports.

TIRANA

Berati

Population:	**3.2 million**
Money:	**Lek**
Language:	**Albanian**
Hello:	**Mire dite**
Pronunciation:	**meer-dee-tah**

Malta

The barren rocky island of Malta has some of the oldest buildings in the world. There are many religious festivals celebrated with music, fireworks and processions.

VALLETTA

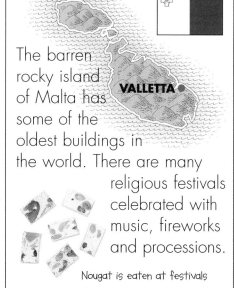

Nougat is eaten at festivals

Population:	**393,000**
Money:	**Maltese lira**
Language:	**Maltese**
Hello:	**Merhba**
Pronunciation:	**mehr-hah-bah**

Istanbul's Grand Covered Bazaar is a maze of streets with over 3,000 shops

Turkey's position between Asia and Europe has led to a mix of architectural styles

Population:	**68.6 million**
Money:	**Turkish lira**
Language:	**Turkish**
Hello:	**Merhaba**
Pronunciation:	**MARE-huh-buh**

Russian Federation

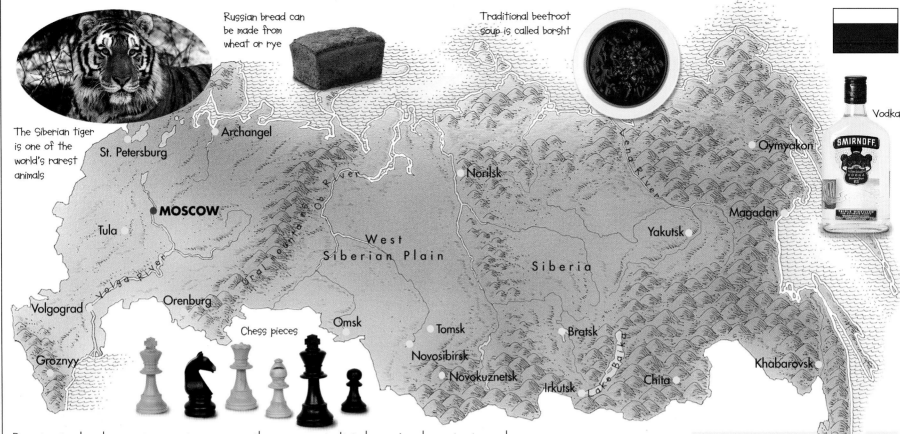

The Siberian tiger is one of the world's rarest animals

Russian bread can be made from wheat or rye

Traditional beetroot soup is called borsht

Vodka

Archangel

St. Petersburg

MOSCOW

Tula

Orenburg

Volgograd

Groznyy

Omsk

Tomsk

Novosibirsk

Novokuznetsk

Irkutsk

Norilsk

West Siberian Plain

Siberia

Bratsk

Chita

Yakutsk

Magadan

Oymyakon

Khabarovsk

Vladivostok

Chess pieces

Russia is the largest country on earth, although it is only seventh largest in population terms. It is about 9,600 km wide and spans 11 time zones. Kalingrad is a part of Russia, but is separated from the rest of the country by Lithuania and Latvia. The Ural Mountains divide Russia: to the west, the country is in Europe, to the east, it is in Asia. 80% of the population live in the European part of Russia. The Trans-Siberian Railway links Moscow in the west and Vladivostok in the east. It takes six days to travel between the two. The railway is vital for trade and communication. Much of Russia is empty grassland or forest. Siberia has the largest forest in the world, home to elk, brown bear and sable. Russia also has the world's deepest lake, Lake Baikal, which contains one quarter of the world's fresh water. Scientists have calculated that it would take one year for all the rivers in the world to fill the lake.

The ballet schools in St Petersburg and Moscow are world famous

Famous for...

Space exploration
Yuri Gagarin was the first person in space. He orbited the Earth in 1961

Caviar
These fish eggs are considered a great delicacy and are served on buckwheat pancakes

Chess
Many of the world's greatest chess players have been Russian

Vodka
A strong alcoholic liquor made by distilling grain or potatoes

Ballet
Enjoyed by people of all ages

Population:	**143 million**
Money:	**Russian rouble**
Language:	**Russian**
Hello:	**Zdravstvuite**
Pronunciation:	**zzDRAST-vet-yah**

Russian Orthodox churches, like St. Basil's Cathedral, have onion-shaped domes

The brown bear, found all over Russia, is the country's national symbol

Catherine's Palace in Pushkin, near St. Petersburg, is one of Russia's finest buildings

Kazakhstan

High, grassy plains cover most of the country, with mountains in the east. Gerbils come from the sandy deserts in the south – they are much bigger than those kept as pets.

Population:	**16 million**
Money:	**Tenge**
Language:	**Kazakh**
Hello:	**Salom**
Pronunciation:	**sah-LAHM**

Uzbekistan

The inland Aral Sea is shrinking due to water taken for cotton crops. It has lost 75% of its water, changing the local climate. Cotton is one of the largest exports.

Population:	**25.6 million**
Money:	**Som**
Language:	**Uzbek**
Hello:	**Salaam a'alaykum**
Pronunciation:	**sah-LAHM ah ah-LAY-koom**

Kyrgyzstan

Much of this high, mountainous country is under permanent snow, but Lake Issyk-Kul is slightly salty and never freezes. Snow leopards are found in the wild.

Snow leopard

Population:	**5 million**
Money:	**Som**
Language:	**Kyrgyz**
Hello:	**Salaam**
Pronunciation:	**sah-LAHM**

Tajikistan

Tajikistan experiences both winter snow storms and summer dust storms. Wolves live on the lower parts of the mountain ranges.

Wolf

Population:	**6.2 million**
Money:	**Somoni**
Language:	**Tajik**
Hello:	**Salom**
Pronunciation:	**sah-LOM**

Georgia

The varied countryside makes Georgia a popular holiday destination. There are beaches, snow-covered mountains and grassy plains full of flowers.

Lemons, limes and apricots are grown here

Population:	**5.2 million**
Money:	**Lari**
Language:	**Georgian**
Hello:	**Gamarjobet**
Pronunciation:	**gah-mar-joh-baht**

Armenia

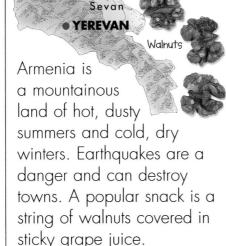

Walnuts

Armenia is a mountainous land of hot, dusty summers and cold, dry winters. Earthquakes are a danger and can destroy towns. A popular snack is a string of walnuts covered in sticky grape juice.

Population:	**3.8 million**
Money:	**Dram**
Language:	**Armenian**
Hello:	**Parev**
Pronunciation:	**bar-ev**

Turkmenistan

Turkmenistan has very few inhabitants for its size, due to four-fifths of the land being inhospitable desert. In the Kugitang Mountains you can see dinosaur footprints.

Population:	**4.9 million**
Money:	**Manat**
Language:	**Turkmen**
Hello:	**Salaam**
Pronunciation:	**sah-LAHM**

Azerbaijan

This small country has been exporting oil for many years. The first-ever oil pipeline was built here – it was made of wood.

Population:	**8.1 million**
Money:	**Manat**
Language:	**Azerbaijani**
Hello:	**Salam**
Pronunciation:	**sah-LAHM**

Iran

Iran is a mountainous country with active volcanoes. Earthquakes are a natural hazard. It is also very windy. Summer winds can reach up to 100 km per hour. Iran has a huge salt waste (320 km long) which is unexplored due to the treacherous terrain. Iran is famous for its carpets, made here since the 5th century BC.

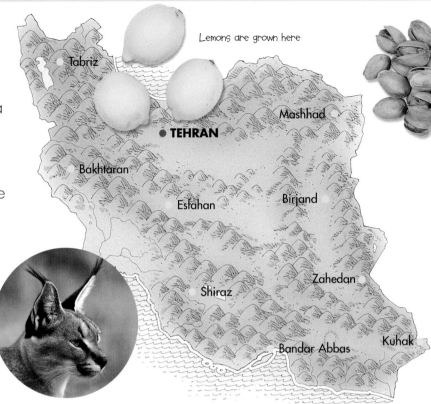

Lemons are grown here

Tabriz

Mashhad

● TEHRAN

Bakhtaran

Esfahan

Birjand

Shiraz

Zahedan

Bandar Abbas

Kuhak

Pistachio nuts are a major Iranian crop

Women in Iran wearing a traditional Islamic dress called a burkha

The citadel, part of the huge mud city of Bam, in southeastern Iran

Wild cats live in Iran's deserts and mountains

Population:	70 million
Money:	Iranian rial
Language:	Farsi
Hello:	Sa'lem
Pronunciation:	sah-LEM

Israel

Israel is a small country which has fertile valleys, beautiful beaches, dusty deserts and rolling hills. It has influenced every corner of the world since it is the Holy Land for Jews, Christians and Muslims. Only 25% of the people living in Israel were born there. The rest come from over 100 different countries, so signs in shops are often in many different languages.

Nazareth

West Bank

Tel Aviv

JERUSALEM

Gaza Strip

Dead Sea

Eilat

Famous for...

Dead Sea
At 400 metres below sea level, this is the lowest point in the world. This sea has eight times more salt in it than the oceans

Jewish holy sites
Tourists from all over the world travel here to see sites such as the Wailing Wall and the remains of Solomon's Temple

Population:	6.3 million
Money:	Shekel
Language:	Hebrew
Hello:	Shalom
Pronunciation:	sha-LOHM

The Dome of the Rock Mosque, on Temple Mount in the city of Jerusalem

Oranges are grown here and exported all over the world

Palestine

There are two areas within Israel that are run by the Palestinians. They would like the West Bank and the Gaza Strip to be recognized as a separate country.

West Bank

Jericho

JERUSALEM ●

Bethlehem

Gaza

Gaza Strip

Population:	3.5 million
Money:	Jordanian dinar
Language:	Arabic
Hello:	Salaam a'alaykum
Pronunciation:	sah-LAHM ah ah-LAY-koom

Iraq

Most of Iraq is desert, but two main rivers, the Tigris and the Euphrates, flow through the country. This area – known as Mesopotamia – was home to the first civilizations to develop in human history. It was here people first lived in towns and developed writing. According to the Bible, the Garden of Eden was said to exist between the Euphrates and Tigris rivers. Today, the fertile land between the two rivers is used to grow dates and cotton. Iraq is one of the world's largest producers of dates.

Fresh dates

The Iraqi capital, Baghdad, has many old mosques and other sacred buildings

Date palms grow in the fertile valleys alongside the Tigris and Euphrates Rivers

Population:	24.2 million
Money:	Iraqi dinar
Language:	Arabic
Hello:	Salaam a'alaykum
Pronunciation:	sah-LAHM ah ah-LAY-koom

Saudi Arabia

Saudi Arabia is a dry desert land, ruled by the Saud Ibn Saud family. It has a quarter of the world's oil reserves which has made the country very wealthy. Mohammed, the founder of the religion of Islam, was born in Mecca. Every year, 2 million Muslim pilgrims travel to Mecca. Over 20,000 buses are needed to transport the pilgrims around the country.

The Muslim pilgrimage to Mecca is the world's largest annual religious gathering

Much of Saudi Arabia is covered with vast desert sand dunes

Population:	21.7 million
Money:	Saudi riyal
Language:	Arabic
Hello:	Salaam a'alaykum
Pronunciation:	sah-LAHM ah ah-LAY-koom

Syria

Historically, Syria was on a key trading route, and was therefore invaded many times. Today you can see the ruins left by the various empires – one of the most famous is the Roman city of Palmyra. The world's first alphabet was developed at Ugarit. Desert sandstorms are a natural hazard. 40% of the population is under 15.

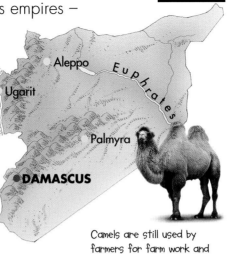

Camels are still used by farmers for farm work and pulling carts to market

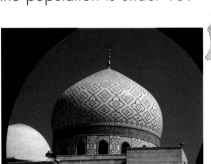

The dome of the Sayyida Ruqayya Mosque in the Syrian capital, Damascus

Population:	17 million
Money:	Syrian pound
Language:	Arabic
Hello:	Salaam a'alaykum
Pronunciation:	sah-LAHM ah ah-LAY-koom

Bahrain

Bahrain is a group of 34 islands. Much of its money comes from oil refining. Most food is imported.

Many wading birds such as the greater flamingo, live in the shallow waters around the islands

Population:	663,000
Money:	Bahraini dinar
Language:	Arabic
Hello:	Salaam a'alaykum
Pronunciation:	sah-LAHM ah ah-LAY-koom

Jordan

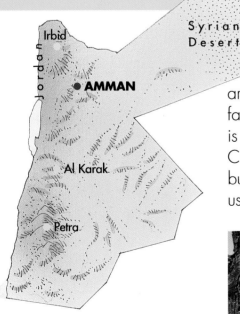

Most of Jordan is desert. There are few trees and not much farmland. The Jordan River is considered a holy river by Christians. Many churches buy water from the river to use at christenings.

The pink city of Petra was carved into solid rock 2,000 years ago

Population:	5.2 million
Money:	Jordanian dinar
Language:	Arabic
Hello:	Salaam a'alaykum
Pronunciation:	sah-LAHM ah ah-LAY-koom

United Arab Emirates (U.A.E)

The United Arab Emirates is divided into seven regions, each ruled by a sheik. The discovery of oil has made this an incredibly wealthy area.

Population:	2.7 million
Money:	UAE dirham
Language:	Arabic
Hello:	Salaam a'alaykum
Pronunciation:	sah-LAHM ah ah-LAY-koom

Yemen

Yemen is mostly desert, hot and dry in the east, hot and humid along the coast. Since Yemen has virtually no fresh water, the people depend on water from oases. Dried and salted fish is an important export.

SANA
Mukalla
Aden

Population:	19.9 million
Money:	**Yemeni rial**
Language:	**Arabic**
Hello:	**Salaam a'alaykum**
Pronunciation:	**sah-LAHM ah ah-LAY-koom**

Afghanistan

Afghanistan has few railways or roads and the rivers are not suitable for boats, so all sorts of pack animals are used to transport goods through the fertile valleys, over the mountains and across the desert plains. Most Afghans are farmers, growing just enough fruit, vegetables and cereals to feed their families.

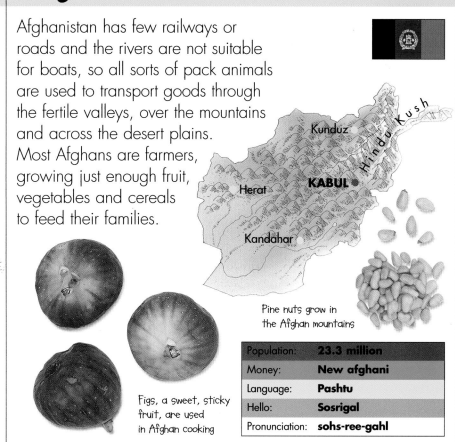

Kunduz
Hindu Kush
Herat
KABUL
Kandahar

Pine nuts grow in the Afghan mountains

Figs, a sweet, sticky fruit, are used in Afghan cooking

Population:	23.3 million
Money:	**New afghani**
Language:	**Pashtu**
Hello:	**Sosrigal**
Pronunciation:	**sohs-ree-gahl**

Kuwait

Kuwait has a flat, gravelly desert. Water has to be pumped from deep in the ground or else taken from the sea. The seawater has to go through a process to make it suitable for drinking or watering crops.

Al Bahrah
KUWAIT CITY
Al Wafra

Fresh water is a precious liquid

Population:	2 million
Money:	**Kuwaiti dollar**
Language:	**Arabic**
Hello:	**Salaam a'alaykum**
Pronunciation:	**sah-LAHM ah ah-LAY-koom**

Oman

MUSCAT

Dates

Salalah

Oman is ruled by a sultan. Its main export is oil. Dates, limes and nuts are grown. Oman has many rare animals, including the giant sea turtle which can grow over 2 metres in length.

Population:	2.7 million
Money:	**Omani rial**
Language:	**Arabic**
Hello:	**Salaam a'alaykum**
Pronunciation:	**sah-LAHM ah ah-LAY-koom**

Lebanon

Lebanon is one of the world's smallest countries – only 170 km long and 50 km wide. Its high mountains are home to the cedar of Lebanon, a type of giant mountain tree famous for its wonderful wood. People have lived in Byblos for about 9,000 years, making it one of the oldest cities in the world.

Tripoli
Byblos
BEIRUT

A tasty snack of hummus and falafel

Golden and imperial eagles live in the mountains of Lebanon

Population:	3.6 million
Money:	**Lats**
Language:	**Arabic**
Hello:	**Salaam a'alaykum**
Pronunciation:	**sah-LAHM ah ah-LAY-koom**

Qatar

Al Khawr
DOHA

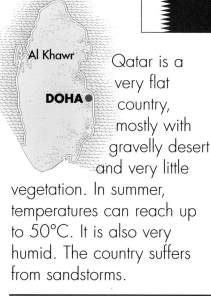

Qatar is a very flat country, mostly with gravelly desert and very little vegetation. In summer, temperatures can reach up to 50°C. It is also very humid. The country suffers from sandstorms.

Population:	584,000
Money:	**Qatari riyal**
Language:	**Arabic**
Hello:	**Salaam a'alaykum**
Pronunciation:	**sah-LAHM ah ah-LAY-koom**

India

India is a huge country with the second largest population in the world. The mixture of peoples and religions in the country means that more than 24 languages are spoken here. There is incredible variety within India, from bustling cities to remote farming villages, and from snow-capped mountains to vast forests and hot plains. Most of India has three seasons in a year – hot, wet and cool. The Ganges is the sacred river of the Hindus. Indians get food from it, travel and transport goods on it, wash laundry and bathe in it and the dead are cremated along its banks.

India's national animal, the tiger, can still be found in some dense forests, although it is endangered

Famous for...

Cricket
India's cricket team is respected all over the world

Temples
There are many beautifully carved Hindu, Sikh and Jain temples

Sacred cows
Cows are sacred in India so you'll see them everywhere

Bollywood
Mumbai is home to the 'Bollywood' film industry.

More films are made here than in Hollywood. They attract large audiences and the actors are huge stars

Curry
Everyone eats curry, even for breakfast!

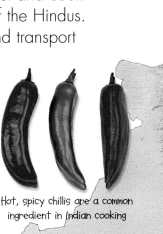

Hot, spicy chillis are a common ingredient in Indian cooking

India is the largest tea producer in the world

Over 9 million people live in Mumbai, making it one of the largest cities in the world

The Taj Mahal is India's most famous building. It took 20,000 people to build it

Many women wear a sari wrapped around their body and draped over their shoulder

Indian cooking uses many spices to flavour the dishes

NEW DELHI

Jaipur
Kanpur
Ganges
Varanasi
Imphal

Vadodara
Bhopal
Kolkata (Calcutta)

Surat
Nagpur

Mumbai (Bombay)
Vishakhapatnam

Hyderabad

Andaman Islands

Chennai (Madras)

Arabian Sea
Bangalore

Indian Ocean

Nicobar Islands

Population:	1.04 billion
Money:	Indian rupee
Language:	Hindi
Hello:	Namaste
Pronunciation:	nah-mah-STAY

Pakistan

Pakistani drivers like to decorate their vehicles in bright colours

Leather footballs are made in Pakistan

Pakistan is a dry country with rocky deserts and huge mountains, including K2, the second highest in the world. Most people live near the Indus River where they can grow crops. Pakistan grows a lot of cotton. The cotton seeds are picked by hand. Pakistan exports raw cotton as well as cotton thread, fabric and clothes.

K2, regarded as one of the world's hardest mountains to climb, is in northern Pakistan

Population:	**149 million**
Money:	**Pakistani rupee**
Language:	**Urdu**
Hello:	**Salaam**
Pronunciation:	**sah-LAHM**

Nepal

Tourists come to Nepal to see Mount Everest. Many herbs used in medicines are found on the slopes of Nepal's mountains.

At 8,848 metres high, Mount Everest is the tallest mountain in the world

Population:	**24.2 million**
Money:	**Nepalese rupee**
Language:	**Nepali**
Hello:	**Namaste**
Pronunciation:	**nah-mah-STAY**

Bangladesh

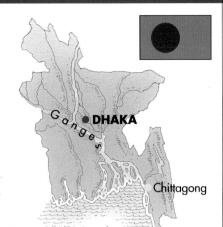

Ganges • **DHAKA**

Chittagong

Bangladesh often experiences terrible floods because of its huge rivers and flat land. The plains are perfect for growing rice.

Population:	**143 million**
Money:	**Taka**
Language:	**Bengali**
Hello:	**Kamon achho**
Pronunciation:	**kay-mohn-ach-hoh**

Sri Lanka

Over 300,000 tons of tea are produced here every year. Known as the 'Island of Gems', precious stones are mined, cut and made into jewellery.

Mannar

• **COLOMBO**

Elephants are popular with tourists

Population:	**19.3 million**
Money:	**Sri Lanka rupee**
Language:	**Sinhala**
Hello:	**Ayubowan**
Pronunciation:	**ah-you-bo-wahng**

Bhutan

The name Bhutan means 'Thunder Dragon', after the storms that come off the Himalayas. The people keep yaks for their meat and milk. Yak dung is also used as fuel.

H i m a l a y a s

• **THIMPHU**

Population:	**2.05 million**
Money:	**Ngultrum**
Language:	**Dzongkha**
Hello:	**Kuzug zangpo**
Pronunciation:	**koo-zoog-jahng-poh**

Maldives

Reefs teeming with brightly coloured fish attract tourists. Global warming is a hazard, as no island is higher than 2.5 metres above sea level.

• **MALÉ**

Tourists come here for the white, sandy beaches

Population:	**309,000**
Money:	**Rufiyaa**
Language:	**Dhivehi**
Hello:	**Salaam a'aalaykum**
Pronunciation:	**sah-LAHM ah ah-LAY-koom**

Myanmar

This very hot, tropical country has many natural resources. Timber, especially teak, and precious stones are the most important. Its rubies are considered to be the finest in the world. Sugarcane juice is a popular drink here.

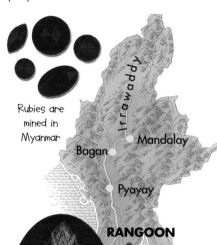

Rubies are mined in Myanmar

Mandalay
Bagan
Pyayay
RANGOON

A Buddhist statue in the Mandalay Palace

The Htilominlo Buddhist Temple in Bagan is one of many throughout Myanmar

Population:	49 million
Money:	Kyat
Language:	Burmese
Hello:	Mingalar pa
Pronunciation:	ming-a-lah pa

Laos

Luang Prabang
Pak Lai
VIENTIANE
Rice
Mukdahan
Mekong

The huge Mekong River is the main route through the mountains and forests. Water buffalo are used for heavy farm work and provide milk and meat. Coffee, tea and rice are grown on mountain plateaus.

Population:	5.5 million
Money:	New kip
Language:	Loa
Hello:	Sabai dee
Pronunciation:	sah-bie-dee

Cambodia

Most Cambodians live by the huge Mekong River which often floods, making the soil perfect for growing rice.

Angkor
Mekong
PHNOM PENH

Population:	13.8 million
Money:	Riel
Language:	Khmer
Hello:	Jimripsu
Pronunciation:	jihm-rihp-soo-ah

Thailand

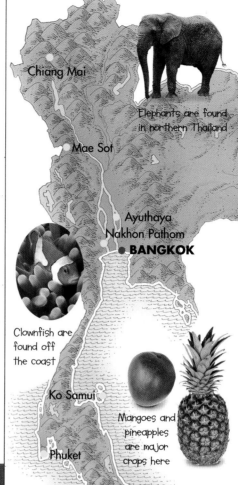

Chiang Mai
Mae Sot
Elephants are found in northern Thailand
Ayuthaya
Nakhon Pathom
BANGKOK
Clownfish are found off the coast
Ko Samui
Mangoes and pineapples are major crops here
Phuket

Thailand is a hot and humid country covered in forests and paddy fields. Tantalum, produced in Thailand, is used in game consoles, mobile phones and laptop computers. There are 1,000 different species of butterfly in Thailand. One of the most beautiful is the Golden Birdwing butterfly.

Longtail boats are used for fishing and diving and as ferries in the seas around Thailand

These women are making flower garlands. They are displayed during religious festivals

Many tourists come to Thailand for the beautiful scenery and great beaches

Famous for...

Tuk-tuks
These motorised rickshaws are perfect for travelling through busy cities

Thai food
Spicy and distinctive, usually featuring garlic, chilli, lime and coconut

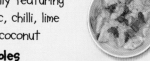

Temples
There are many beautiful Buddhist temples throughout the country

Population:	64.3 million
Money:	Baht
Language:	Thai
Hello:	Sawatdi khap
Pronunciation:	sa-wa-DEE Krab

Malaysia

Malaysia's dense rainforest has many species of plants and animals, including the world's largest and smelliest flower, the rafflesia flower. Some plants are used by drug companies to make medicines. The largest export is computer chips, used in electronic goods. Kite flying is a popular pastime.

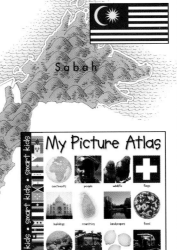

Many books are printed in Malaysia, including this one

For many years the Petronas Towers were the world's tallest buildings (452 metres high)

Latex from the rubber tree is used to make tyres and keypads for remote controls

Population:	23 million
Money:	Ringgit
Language:	Malay
Hello:	Selamet pagi
Pronunciation:	seh-LA-maht PAH-gee

Singapore

Singapore is a tiny, wealthy country with a busy port. It is one of the most crowded countries in the world, but it is also very clean. Anyone who drops litter must pay a large fine.

Population:	4.2 million
Money:	Singapore dollar
Language:	Chinese
Hello:	Ni hao
Pronunciation:	nee haOW

Indonesia

Indonesia is made up of 17,000 islands with soaring mountains, dense jungles, white, sandy beaches and active volcanoes. It is the largest group of islands in the world and stretches 5,000 km from the Indian Ocean to the Pacific Ocean. It is also the world's largest Muslim country and there are more than 580 different languages spoken here.

The climate is ideal for growing all sorts of exotic, tasty fruit, including the thorny durian. It smells horrible but it tastes delicious.

Sweet papaya is grown in Indonesia

Orangutans are under threat as their forest habitat is chopped down for timber

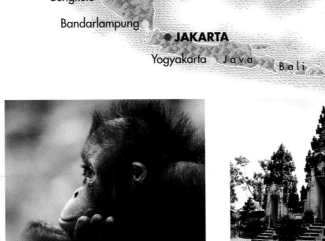

There are many ancient Hindu temples in Indonesia. This one is on the island of Bali

Population:	218 million
Money:	Rupiah
Language:	Indonesian
Hello:	Selamat pagi
Pronunciation:	seh-LA-maht PAH-gee

Vietnam

Vietnam's large flood plains and hot, wet climate make it an ideal place to grow rice. The rice is planted by hand in specially flooded paddy fields. Vietnam's many rivers and canals provide fish to eat, water for crops and a means to get around. Boats come in all shapes and sizes, some long and thin, others completely round. In the cities, cyclos are a useful means of getting around. These are pedal powered machines that can transport a whole family.

HANOI ●   Haiphong

Vinh

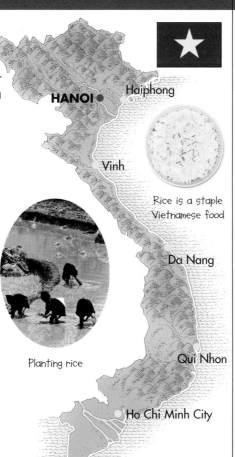

Planting rice

Rice is a staple Vietnamese food

Da Nang

Qui Nhon

Ho Chi Minh City

Market traders load their bicycles with fruit and other goods for sale

Population:	80.2 million
Money:	Dong
Language:	Vietnamese
Hello:	chao
Pronunciation:	chow

Philippines

The Philippines suffers frequent natural disasters such as floods, earthquakes, typhoons and volcanic eruptions.

The Philippines is a group of 7,107 islands

Traditional houses are on stilts to protect families from flooding and wild animals. The Rice Research Institute in Manila breeds new species of rice to help farmers grow more using less land and less water.

Luzon

Dagupan

● MANILA

Rattan baskets are made here

Samar

Panay   Tacloban

Bacolod

Palawan

Mindanao

Zamboanga

General Santos

Filipinos living near an active volcano leave their houses as soon as a warning is given

Population:	78.6 million
Money:	Philippine peso
Language:	English
Hello:	Hello
Pronunciation:	hel-lo

East Timor

East Timor is one of the world's newest countries. It became independent from Indonesia on May 20, 2002. Coffee is East Timor's largest export, but deposits of oil and gas have been found offshore.

Tutuala

● DILI

Coffee beans

Population:	779,000
Money:	US dollar
Language:	Portuguese
Hello:	Bom dia
Pronunciation:	bohn DEE-ah

Brunei

BANDAR SERI BEGAWAN ●

Tutong

Kampong Sukang

Brunei is a tiny Muslim country ruled by a sultan. Its huge reserves of oil and gas have made both the country and the sultan very wealthy.

The Omar Ali Saifuddin Mosque in Bandar Seri Begawan

Population:	341,000
Money:	Brunei dollar
Language:	Malay
Hello:	Selemat pagi
Pronunciation:	seh-LA-maht PAH-gee

China

This enormous country is the third largest in the world. It is also home to more people than any other country on Earth – one-fifth of the world's population is Chinese. The landscape is very varied, from high mountains in the west to plains in the east. Forests can be found in the north, deserts in the centre of the country and rainforests in the south. Many places in China have extremes of temperature – very hot in summer and very cold in winter. Over half of China's population work to grow grain, rice and other important crops. Chinese people from different regions speak different dialects. However, they can all understand the written Chinese language. Instead of an alphabet of different letters, each Chinese word has its own character.

Famous for...

Silk
To make silk, cocoons of the silk moth are dropped in boiling water and the thread unwound. Each cocoon makes over 1 km of silk

Herbal medicines
Many native plants, such as ginseng and ginkgo, are used in traditional Chinese medicine

Inventions
Paper, printing, banknotes, fine pottery, fireworks, gunpowder, the compass, wheelbarrows and umbrellas are all Chinese inventions

Kites
The first kites were made from bamboo and silk about 2,000 years ago

Population:	1.29 billion
Money:	Renminbi
Language:	Chinese
Hello:	Ni hao
Pronunciation:	nee haOW

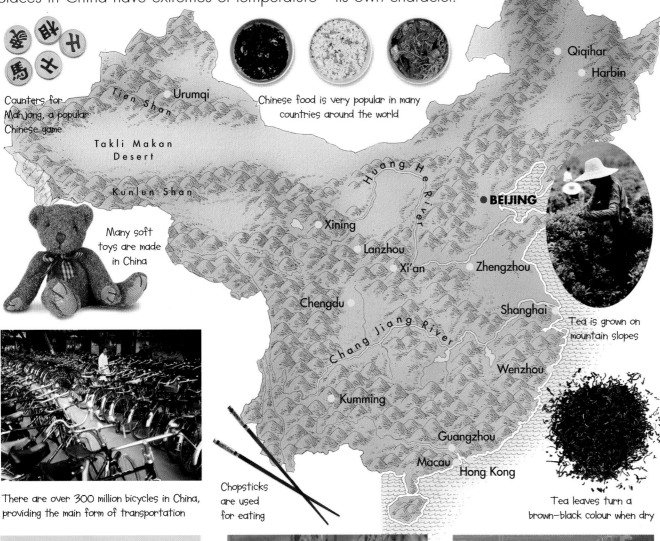

Counters for Mahjong, a popular Chinese game

Chinese food is very popular in many countries around the world

Many soft toys are made in China

Tea is grown on mountain slopes

Tien Shan
Urumqi
Takli Makan Desert
Kunlun Shan
Xining
Lanzhou
Xi'an
Chengdu
Kumming
Huang He River
BEIJING
Zhengzhou
Chang Jiang River
Shanghai
Wenzhou
Guangzhou
Macau
Hong Kong
Qiqihar
Harbin

There are over 300 million bicycles in China, providing the main form of transportation

Chopsticks are used for eating

Tea leaves turn a brown-black colour when dry

The Great Wall of China is 6,000 km long. Some parts were built 2,000 years ago

Giant pandas have to eat for 12 hours a day to get enough nourishment from bamboo

Hong Kong is an important business centre with the world's busiest deep-water port

Tibet

Known as 'the Rooftop of the World', Tibet is set in a plateau high up amidst the Himalayas.

Himalayas
LHASA

Population:	2.6 million
Money:	Renminbi
Language:	Tibetan
Hello:	Tashi delek
Pronunciation:	tah-shi de-leh

Mongolia

Horses are an extremely important part of everyday life in Mongolia

The 'Land of Blue Sky' has very little rain or snow but winters are long and very cold. Most Mongolians are nomadic herdsmen, living in round, white, felt tents, keeping herds of goats, sheep, horses and cattle. They are very proficient on horseback. The children learn to ride before they learn to walk.

Population:	**2.6 million**
Money:	**Tugrik**
Language:	**Mongolian**
Hello:	**Sain Bainuu**
Pronunciation:	**sain bai-nau**

Taiwan

Taiwan has mountain peaks, coastlines of black volcanic rock and misty waterfalls. It also has lively cities, teeming with cars, motorbikes and people. DVDs, TVs, hairdryers and vacuum cleaners are just a few of the electrical products made here and exported around the world.

DVDs and CDs are among the high-tech products made in Taiwan

The National Palace Museum in Taipei holds a large collection of artefacts

Population:	**22.5 million**
Money:	**Taiwan dollar**
Language:	**Chinese**
Hello:	**Ni hao**
Pronunciation:	**nee haOW**

North Korea

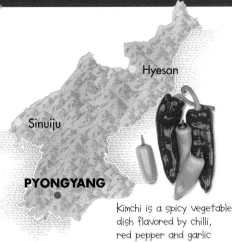

The rugged mountains of North Korea are covered in dense forests, making agriculture difficult, so Koreans have reclaimed land along the coast to grow grain and rice. Mining is important in North Korea. One of the most important minerals mined here is tungsten. Tungsten has the highest melting point of all metals and is used to make lightbulb filaments.

Kimchi is a spicy vegetable dish flavored by chilli, red pepper and garlic

North Korean schoolchildren playing a type of harp called a kayagum

Population:	22.6 million
Money:	North Korean won
Language:	Korean
Hello:	Annyong ha shimnikka
Pronunciation:	an-YOH HASHim-ni-kah

South Korea

The seas around South Korea teem with life, so fishing is an important industry. Koreans process seaweed, extracting chemicals that are used in foods, cosmetics and clothes. South Korea is the largest producer of computer chips in the world. The biggest holiday is on September 12, when Koreans visit the graves of their ancestors.

Seafood

Seaweed is widely eaten

Boats of all sizes are built here, including oil tankers, fishing trawlers and passenger liners

Population:	47.4 million
Money:	South Korean won
Language:	Korean
Hello:	Annyong ha shimnikka
Pronunciation:	an-YOH HASHim-ni-kah

Japan is known as 'the Land of the Rising Sun' and it is one of the richest countries in the world. There are many successful high-tech businesses making cars, televisions and computer games. Tokyo is a major financial center. Active volcanoes and tsunamis (huge waves over 6 metres high) cause a lot of damage. Japan also has about 1,000 earthquakes a year, so earthquake resistant buildings are very important. Shinto is the traditional religion of Japan. People worship the sacred spirits in the form of the sun, mountains, trees, and rocks. Japan is the world leader in the production of computer games. They have designed and developed video and computer games for over 20 years and the leading manufacturers are all based here.

Motorcycles and cars are made in Japan

Flower-viewing picnics are held in April and May, when the cherry trees are in blossom

The Kinkaku-Ji Temple in Kyoto is a beautiful Buddhist temple

Mount Fuji is a sacred mountain in the Shinto religion

Map labels: Hokkaido, Sapporo, Akita, Sendai, Niigata, Honshu, Mt. Fuji, TOKYO, Yokohama, Shizuoka, Kyoto, Nagoya, Kobe, Osaka, Hiroshima, Shikoku, Kochi, Fukuoka, Kyushu

Martial arts have always been popular

The traditional sport of sumo wrestling

'Bullet trains' travel up to 300 kilometres per hour. They are clean and efficient

Much of Tokyo was rebuilt after the 1923 earthquake and the Second World War

Famous for...

Fishing
The Japanese catch – and eat – more fish than any other country in the world

Sushi
Beautifully presented raw fish is a popular dish

Sumo wrestling
Wrestlers try to make their opponents touch the floor. These athletes eat a huge amount of food to add bulk to their bodies

Kimono
A robe with wide sleeves fastened with a sash

Computers and games
The world leader in the development of computer games

Technology
Many new products, such as digital cameras, were invented or improved here

Population:	**128 million**
Money:	**Yen**
Language:	**Japanese**
Hello:	**Konichiwa**
Pronunciation:	**koh-NEE-cheewah**

Australia

This is the world's largest island, measuring 4,000 km across. 65% of the country is 'outback' – flat plains that are some of the hottest and driest places on earth. Most people live in towns and cities along the southern and eastern coasts. The Great Dividing Range Mountains separate these fertile areas from the drier climate inland. Australia is one of the world leaders in mining. It exports more coal than any other country and is one of the world's largest exporters of gold and diamonds. Australia also mines the minerals used in making aluminium. High-tech farming means that Australia is almost entirely self-sufficient. Huge cattle and sheep farms produce dairy products, meat and wool. A quarter of the world's wool is produced here. Outdoor sports are popular in Australia, particularly sailing, surfing, rugby and cricket.

Marsupials
Kangaroos, koalas and possums are found nowhere else on earth. They are unique because their young are carried in pouches

Duck-billed platypus
This strange-looking animal has a tail like a beaver and a beak like a duck. It has fur like a mammal but lays eggs like a bird

Great Barrier Reef
Made from living coral, this is the largest living thing on Earth. It is over 2,000 km long. Thousands of species of fish live here

Dangerous wildlife
Sharks and crocodiles occasionally attack people, but more dangerous are the poisonous snakes and spiders that can be found throughout Australia

Flying doctors
Some people live hundreds of kilometres from the nearest hospital. In an emergency, doctors and medicine are flown to them

Uluru
This massive sandstone block is a sacred Aboriginal site. It is 10 km round and 350 metres high. Thousands of tourists visit it each year

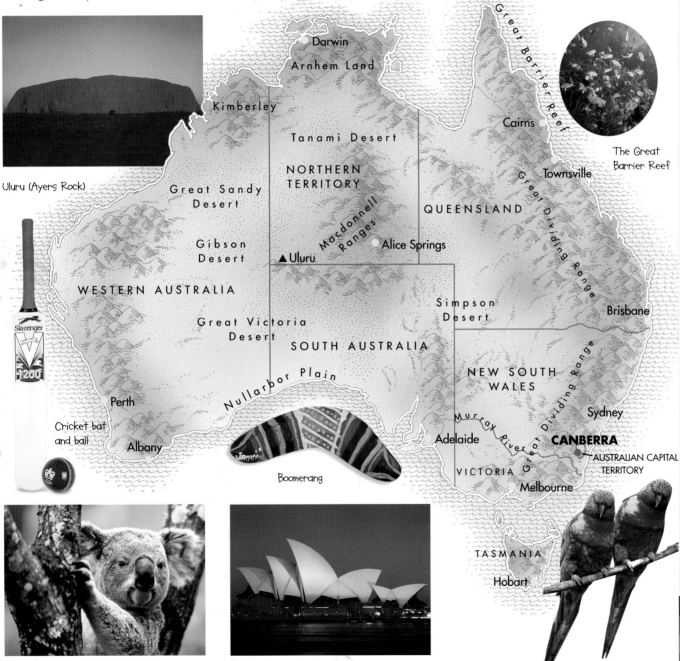

Uluru (Ayers Rock)

Cricket bat and ball

Boomerang

The Great Barrier Reef

Koalas are a protected species, but they are threatened by habitat loss

The uniquely shaped Sydney Opera House is one of the busiest arts centres in the world

Colourful birds can be found in many parts of the country

Darwin
Arnhem Land
Kimberley
Tanami Desert
NORTHERN TERRITORY
Great Barrier Reef
Cairns
Townsville
Great Sandy Desert
Gibson Desert
Macdonnell Ranges
Uluru
Alice Springs
QUEENSLAND
Great Dividing Range
WESTERN AUSTRALIA
Great Victoria Desert
Simpson Desert
Brisbane
SOUTH AUSTRALIA
Perth
Nullarbor Plain
Albany
NEW SOUTH WALES
Sydney
Murray River
Adelaide
CANBERRA
AUSTRALIAN CAPITAL TERRITORY
VICTORIA
Melbourne
TASMANIA
Hobart

Population:	**19.5 million**
Money:	**Australian dollar**
Language:	**English**
Hello:	**Hello**
Pronunciation:	**hel-lo**

78

Kiribati

● BAIRIKI

Kiribati is a group of 33 tiny tropical coral islands. The people fish, farm seaweed and grow coconuts.

Population:	**96,400**
Money:	**Australian dollar**
Language:	**English**
Hello:	**Hello**
Pronunciation:	**hel-lo**

Tuvalu

There are no rivers on these nine islands, so the people collect and store rainwater. **FONGAFALE** The only crop grown for export is coconuts.

Population:	**11,200**
Money:	**Tuvaluan dollar**
Language:	**English**
Hello:	**Hello**
Pronunciation:	**hel-lo**

Nauru

At just 20 square km, this is the smallest republic in the world. There is no capital city.

Population:	**12,300**
Money:	**Australian dollar**
Language:	**Nauruan**
Hello:	**A kamawirei**
Pronunciation:	**a kam-a-wir-ay**

Palau

Palau has six main island groups totaling over 300 islands. Tourists come to see the spectacular sea life including giant clams.

OREOR

Population:	19,400
Money:	US dollar
Language:	English
Hello:	Hello
Pronunciation:	hel-lo

Marshall Islands

This country consists of over 1,000 coral islands. All of the world's species of turtle are found in the seas here.

MAJURO

Population:	73,630
Money:	US dollar
Language:	English
Hello:	Hello
Pronunciation:	hel-lo

Vanuatu

These 80 islands are mountainous with active volcanoes. The land is covered in tropical forests.

PORT-VILA

Population:	207,000
Money:	Vatu
Language:	English
Hello:	Hello
Pronunciation:	hel-lo

Tonga

Only 40 of the 170 islands of Tonga are inhabited. Most of these tropical islands are covered in lush rainforest. Farming is the most important industry, and the main export crops are pumpkins, coconuts, vanilla pods and bananas. It is the only monarchy in the Pacific.

NUKU'ALOFA

Vanilla pods and coconuts are grown here

Population:	106,000
Money:	Pa'anga-Tongan dollar
Language:	English
Hello:	Hello
Pronunciation:	hel-lo

Samoa

The islands of Savi'i and Upolu are hilly with dense rainforest. Most people in rural areas are self-sufficient, growing crops and fishing for food. The main exports are hardwood timber and coconut cream.

Savai'i

Upolu

APIA

Rugby is a popular sport on the islands

Population:	177,000
Money:	Tala
Language:	English
Hello:	Hello
Pronunciation:	hel-lo

Micronesia

Yap Islands

PALIKIR

The name Micronesia means 'small islands' and is appropriate for this group of 607 islands. Exports include fish, black pepper and craft items. Oysters are farmed to produce pearls. On Yap, stone money is still used.

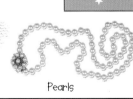

Pearls

Population:	136,000
Money:	US dollar
Language:	English
Hello:	Hello
Pronunciation:	hel-lo

Solomon Islands

This country is spread across 998 islands. The six main islands are mountainous and covered in dense rainforests. Forestry is the main industry, and timber the main export. The valuable wood is used for boatbuilding and flooring. There are active volcanoes and frequent earth tremors.

● HONIARA

Shells are sold abroad and used to make buttons

Population:	479,000
Money:	Solomon Islands dollar
Language:	English
Hello:	Hello
Pronunciation:	hel-lo

Fiji

The 100 inhabited islands of Fiji are covered in forests or grassy plains. The people grow yams and rice to eat. Fiji also has 700 uninhabited islands, most of which are surrounded by coral reef. Tourists come here to see the huge shoals of colourful tropical fish.

Dolphins swim in the coral reefs

● SUVA

Population:	832,000
Money:	Fijian dollar
Language:	English
Hello:	Hello
Pronunciation:	hel-lo

Papua New Guinea

Over 1,000 tribes live here, speaking 700 different languages. The largest butterfly in the world – the Queen Alexandra's Birdwing butterfly – is found in Papua New Guinea's rainforests. It often has a wingspan of more than 25 cm.

Wewak

Madang

● PORT MORESBY

Parrots live in the tropical rainforest

Population:	5 million
Money:	Kina
Language:	English
Hello:	Hello
Pronunciation:	hel-lo

New Zealand

The islands of New Zealand are known for their natural beauty. Rotorua is one of Earth's wonders, with hot springs, geysers, bubbling mud pools and coloured lakes and pools. Most people live on North Island and work in the service industries, but agriculture is also very important. Pine forests produce timber for furniture and wood pulp for paper making. Cattle are raised for meat and dairy products. Beef, butter, cheese and milk powder are processed for export.

Auckland

Rotorua

North Island

Palmerston

● WELLINGTON

Blenheim

Southern Alps

Christchurch

South Island

Dunedin

Kiwi fruit

Spectacular waterfall

Tourists come to New Zealand for the beautiful countryside and beaches

Sheep are kept for their meat and their wool which is used to make clothing and carpets

Famous for...

Kiwi bird
This flightless bird is the same size as a chicken, but it lays eggs as big as an ostrich's

Kiwi fruit
This brown, round fruit is said to resemble the kiwi bird

The All Blacks
The national rugby team performs a Maori dance before each match

Population:	**3.8 million**
Money:	**New Zealand dollar**
Language:	**English**
Hello:	**Hello**
Pronunciation:	**hel-lo**

Antarctica

Antarctica was the last continent to be discovered. It is the highest, coldest and windiest continent on Earth. It is covered in a thick layer of ice that is 5 km deep in some places. Antarctica has 90% of all the ice in the world. Air temperatures inland fall to −75°C and rise to −29°C in summer. Winds can be up to 300 kilometres per hour. There is an international agreement to set aside Antarctica for research. Scientists come here to study the land, the sealife and the atmosphere.

Seabirds find plenty of fish in the seas

Lesser Antarctica ● South Pole Greater Antarctica

Seven different species of penguin live and breed on the Antarctic coast

The Antarctic interior supports almost no life. Nothing grows but lichens and moss

Famous for...

Coldest recorded temperature
−89°C

Longest day
On December 21st, there is 24 hours of daylight

Sealife
The seas are full of tiny plants, providing plenty of food for fish

Whales
Seven species of whale live here

Several countries in the world govern places for strategic, economic or political reasons. These are called overseas territories.

Australia

Ashmore and Cartier Island

Population:	0
Money:	None
Language:	English
Hello:	Hello
Pronunciation:	hel-lo

Christmas Island

Population:	500
Money:	Australian dollar
Language:	English
Hello:	Hello
Pronunciation:	hel-lo

Cocos Islands

Population:	600
Money:	Australian dollar
Language:	English
Hello:	Hello
Pronunciation:	hel-lo

Coral Sea Islands

Population:	0
Money:	None
Language:	English
Hello:	Hello
Pronunciation:	hel-lo

Heard and McDonald Island

Population:	0
Money:	None
Language:	English
Hello:	Hello
Pronunciation:	hel-lo

Norfolk Island

Population:	1,900
Money:	Australian dollar
Language:	English
Hello:	Hello
Pronunciation:	hel-lo

Denmark

Faeroe Islands

Population:	46,000
Money:	Danish krone
Language:	Faroese
Hello:	Godan dag
Pronunciation:	goh-dan dagh

Greenland

Population:	56,400
Money:	Danish krone
Language:	Inuttut
Hello:	Aluu
Pronunciation:	ah-loo

France

Clipperton Island

Population:	0
Money:	None
Language:	French
Hello:	Bonjour
Pronunciation:	bohn-ZHOOR

French Guiana

Population:	182,300
Money:	Euro
Language:	French
Hello:	Bonjour
Pronunciation:	bohn-ZHOOR

French Polynesia

Population:	245,400
Money:	Pacific franc
Language:	French
Hello:	Bonjour
Pronunciation:	bohn-ZHOOR

Guadeloupe

Population:	435,000
Money:	Euro
Language:	French
Hello:	Bonjour
Pronunciation:	bohn-ZHOOR

Martinique

Population:	388,000
Money:	Euro
Language:	French
Hello:	Bonjour
Pronunciation:	bohn-ZHOOR

Mayotte

Population:	170,900
Money:	Euro
Language:	French
Hello:	Bonjour
Pronunciation:	bohn-ZHOOR

New Caledonia

Population:	224,000
Money:	Pacific franc
Language:	French
Hello:	Bonjour
Pronunciation:	bohn-ZHOOR

Reunion

Population:	742,000
Money:	Euro
Language:	French
Hello:	Bonjour
Pronunciation:	bohn-ZHOOR

St. Pierre and Miquelon

Population:	6,900
Money:	Euro
Language:	French
Hello:	Bonjour
Pronunciation:	bohn-ZHOOR

Wallia and Futuna

Population:	15,600
Money:	Pacific franc
Language:	French
Hello:	Bonjour
Pronunciation:	bohn-ZHOOR

Netherlands

Aruba

Population:	70,400
Money:	Aruban gulden
Language:	Papiamentu
Hello:	Bon dia
Pronunciation:	bohn-dee-ah

Netherlands Antilles

Population:	219,000
Money:	N'lands Antilles gulden
Language:	Papiamentu
Hello:	Bon dia
Pronunciation:	bohn-dee-ah

New Zealand

Cook Islands

Population:	20,800
Money:	New Zealand dollar
Language:	English
Hello:	Hello
Pronunciation:	hel-lo

Niue

Population:	2,100
Money:	New Zealand dollar
Language:	English
Hello:	Hello
Pronunciation:	hel-lo

Tokelau

Population:	1,400
Money:	New Zealand dollar
Language:	English
Hello:	Hello
Pronunciation:	hel-lo

Norway

Bouvet Island

Population:	0
Money:	None
Language:	Norwegian
Hello:	God dag
Pronunciation:	goo-dagh

Jan Mayen

Population:	0
Money:	None
Language:	Norwegian
Hello:	God dag
Pronunciation:	goo-dagh

Peter I. Island

Population:	0
Money:	None
Language:	Norwegian
Hello:	God dag
Pronunciation:	goo-dagh

Svalbard

Population:	2,800
Money:	Norwegian krone
Language:	Norwegian
Hello:	God dag
Pronunciation:	goo-dagh

United Kingdom

Anguilla

Population:	12,500
Money:	East Caribbean dollar
Language:	English
Hello:	Hello
Pronunciation:	hel-lo

Ascension Island

Population:	980
Money:	St. Helena pound
Language:	English
Hello:	Hello
Pronunciation:	hel-lo

Bermuda

Population:	63,900
Money:	Bermuda dollar
Language:	English
Hello:	Hello
Pronunciation:	hel-lo

British Indian Ocean Territory

Population:	3,500
Money:	US dollar
Language:	English
Hello:	Hello
Pronunciation:	hel-lo

British Virgin Islands

Population:	21,300
Money:	US dollar
Language:	English
Hello:	Hello
Pronunciation:	hel-lo

Cayman Islands

Population:	36,300
Money:	Cayman Islands dollar
Language:	English
Hello:	Hello
Pronunciation:	hel-lo

Falkland Islands

Population:	2,900
Money:	Falklands Islands pound
Language:	English
Hello:	Hello
Pronunciation:	hel-lo

Gibraltar

Population:	27,700
Money:	Gibraltar pound
Language:	English
Hello:	Hello
Pronunciation:	hel-lo

Guernsey

Population:	64,600
Money:	Pound sterling
Language:	English
Hello:	Hello
Pronunciation:	hel-lo

Isle of Man

Population:	73,900
Money:	Pound sterling
Language:	English
Hello:	Hello
Pronunciation:	hel-lo

Jersey

Population:	89,800
Money:	Pound sterling
Language:	English
Hello:	Hello
Pronunciation:	hel-lo

Montserrat

Population:	8,400
Money:	East Caribbean dollar
Language:	English
Hello:	Hello
Pronunciation:	hel-lo

Pitcairn Islands

Population:	50
Money:	Pitcairn dollar
Language:	English
Hello:	Hello
Pronunciation:	hel-lo

South Georgia and the Sandwich Islands

Population:	**0**
Money:	**None**
Language:	**English**
Hello:	**Hello**
Pronunciation:	**hel-lo**

St. Helena

Population:	**4,600**
Money:	**St. Helena pound**
Language:	**English**
Hello:	**Hello**
Pronunciation:	**hel-lo**

Tristan da Cunha

Population:	**300**
Money:	**St. Helena pound**
Language:	**English**
Hello:	**Hello**
Pronunciation:	**hel-lo**

Turks and Caicos Islands

Population:	**18,700**
Money:	**US dollar**
Language:	**English**
Hello:	**Hello**
Pronunciation:	**hel-lo**

USA

American Samoa

Population:	**68,700**
Money:	**US dollar**
Language:	**English**
Hello:	**Hello**
Pronunciation:	**hel-lo**

Baker and Howland Islands

Population:	**0**
Money:	**None**
Language:	**English**
Hello:	**Hello**
Pronunciation:	**hel-lo**

Guam

Population:	**162,000**
Money:	**US dollar**
Language:	**English**
Hello:	**Hello**
Pronunciation:	**hel-lo**

Jarvis Island

Population:	**0**
Money:	**None**
Language:	**English**
Hello:	**Hello**
Pronunciation:	**hel-lo**

Johnston Atoll

Population:	**0**
Money:	**None**
Language:	**English**
Hello:	**Hello**
Pronunciation:	**hel-lo**

Kingman Reef

Population:	**0**
Money:	**None**
Language:	**English**
Hello:	**Hello**
Pronunciation:	**hel-lo**

Midway Islands

Population:	**0**
Money:	**None**
Language:	**English**
Hello:	**Hello**
Pronunciation:	**hel-lo**

Navassa Island

Population:	**0**
Money:	**None**
Language:	**English**
Hello:	**Hello**
Pronunciation:	**hel-lo**

Northern Mariana Islands

Population:	**77,300**
Money:	**US dollar**
Language:	**English**
Hello:	**Hello**
Pronunciation:	**hel-lo**

Palmyra Atoll

Population:	**0**
Money:	**None**
Language:	**English**
Hello:	**Hello**
Pronunciation:	**hel-lo**

Puerto Rico

Population:	**3.9 million**
Money:	**US dollar**
Language:	**English**
Hello:	**Hello**
Pronunciation:	**hel-lo**

Virgin Islands

Population:	**123,500**
Money:	**US dollar**
Language:	**English**
Hello:	**Hello**
Pronunciation:	**hel-lo**

Wake Island

Population:	**0**
Money:	**None**
Language:	**English**
Hello:	**Hello**
Pronunciation:	**hel-lo**

Index

Index

Index

Index

Index

Acknowledgements

Photography: p.18 Steel drums, Oliver Benn (Getty Images), p.20 Quetzal, Ralph Lee Hopkins (Lonely Planet), p.21 Hummingbird, Margarette Mead (Getty Images), p.21 Cars, Trevor Wood (Getty Images), p.21 Havana, Tom Bean (Getty Images), p.22 Bogota, Krzysztof Dydynski (Lonely Planet), p.22 Palacio Salvo, Wayne Walton (Lonely Planet), p.22 Rainforest, Greg Caire (Lonely Planet), p.25 Polo, Phil Weymouth (Lonely Planet), p.42 Oil rig, Mark A. Leman (Getty Images), p.42 Skier, Terje Rakke (Getty Images), p.43 Helsinki, Stephen Saks (Lonely Planet), p.45 Holy Spirit Church, Glen Allison (Getty Images), p.45 Lake, Graeme Cornwallis (Lonely Planet), p.45 Street, Anders Blomqvist (Lonely Planet), p.46 Bicycles, Mark Downey (Getty Images), p.46 The Hague, Andrew Ward (Getty Images), p.46 Windmill, Hindeo Kurihara (Getty Images), p.47 EU, Neil Beer (Getty Images), p.49 TGV, Chris Kapolka (Getty Images) p.52 Ferries, Paul Trummer (Getty Images), p.52 Zakynthos, Steve Outram (Getty Images), p.54 Black Forest, Josef Bek (Getty Images), p.54 Traditional house, Doug Armand (Getty Images), p.56 Austrian Alps, Neil Beer (Getty Images), p.56 Hallstatt (Getty Images), p.57 Prague, Anthony Cassidy (Getty Images), p.57 Warsaw (Getty Images), p.58 Romanian market, Rhonda Gutenberg (Lonely Planet), p.58 St. Andrew's Church, John Noble (Lonely Planet), p.59 Women, Lee Foster (Lonely Planet), p.61 Bazaar, Grant V. Faint (Getty Images) p.61 Carpets, Robert Freck (Getty Images), P.62 Catherine Palace (Getty Images), p.63 Snow leopard, Tim Davis (Getty Images), p.64 Citadel, Thomas Schmitt (Getty Images), p.64 Dead Sea, Hugh Sitton (Getty Images), p.64 Iranian women, John Borthwick (Lonely Planet), p.65 Al-Aqsa, Siqui Sanchez (Getty Images), p.65 Mecca, Nabeel Turner (Getty Images), p.66 Petra, Jon Arnold (Getty Images), p.66 Sayyida Ruqayya Mosque, John Elk III (Lonely Planet), p.68 Mumbai, Eddie Gerald (Lonely Planet), p.69 K2, Ed Darack (Getty Images), p.69 Truck, James Strachan (Getty Images), p.72 Hindu Temples, Dennie Cody (Getty Images), p.72 Petronas Tower, Josef Beck (Getty Images), p.73 Brunei, Robin Smith (Getty Images), p.73 Fruit vendors, Paul Chesley (Getty Images), p.73 Planting rice (Getty Images), p.75 Mongolians, Paul Harris (Getty Images), p.75 Palace Museum, Mark Downey (Getty Images), p.76 Korean children, Tony Wheeler (Lonely Planet), p.77 Sumo wrestlers, Chris Cole (Getty Images).

Additional photography by Richard Brown.

Many thanks to Betty Wass, Jeanne Tabachnick, Herbert Lewis, Earl Gritton and Stephen Volz for the use of their photographs of Africa and to Leonardo for the use of their photographs from tourist boards around the world.

Thanks to the following tourist boards for the use of their photographs: Dominican Republic, Nicaragua, Kenya, Netherlands, Spain, Portugal, Thailand, New Zealand and the Seychelles.

We would also like to thank Penny Boshoff for her research, CIRCA for their data and the CIA for the use of their flags from the World Factbook.

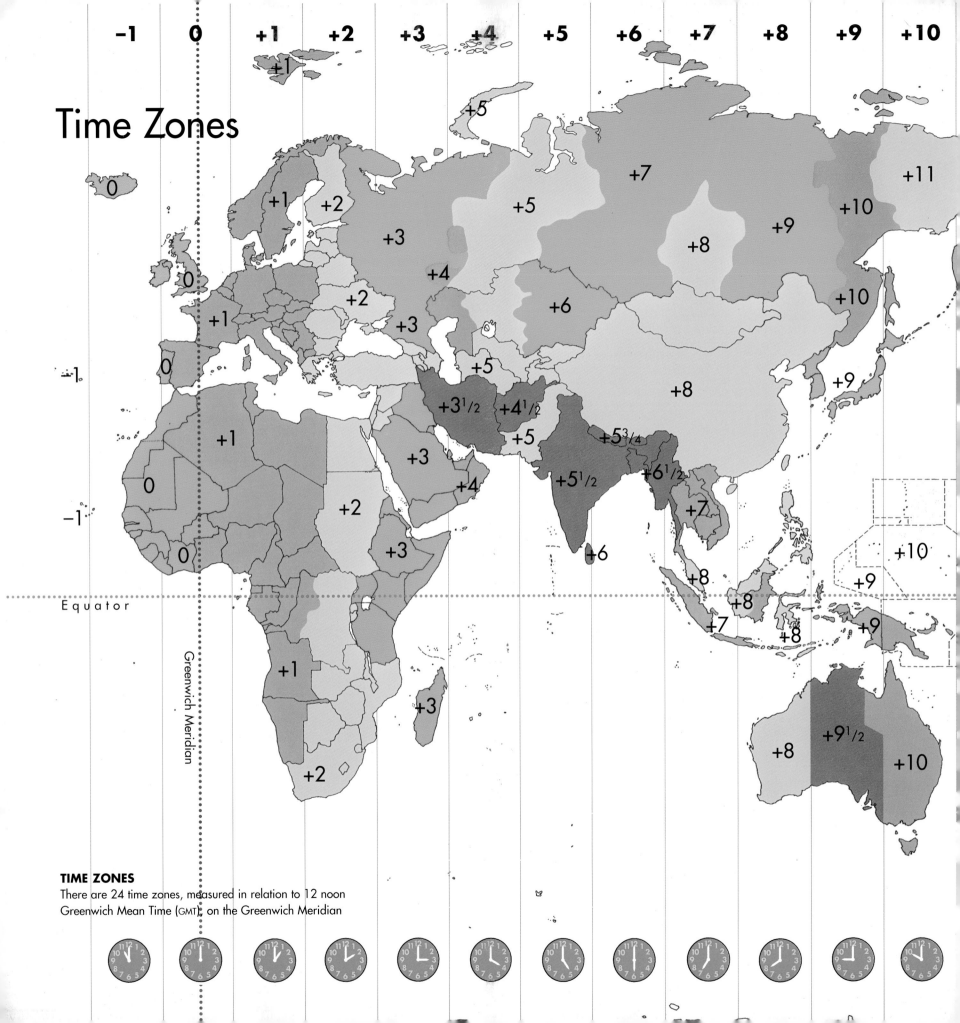

Time Zones

| **−1** | **0** | **+1** | **+2** | **+3** | **+4** | **+5** | **+6** | **+7** | **+8** | **+9** | **+10** |

TIME ZONES
There are 24 time zones, measured in relation to 12 noon
Greenwich Mean Time (GMT), on the Greenwich Meridian

Greenwich Meridian

Equator